MW00456492

THE UNIT

THE UNIT

MY LIFE FIGHTING TERRORISTS AS ONE OF AMERICA'S MOST SECRET MILITARY OPERATIVES

ADAM GAMAL

with KELLY KENNEDY

ST. MARTIN'S PRESS
NEW YORK

First published in the United States by St. Martin's Press,
an imprint of St. Martin's Publishing Group

THE UNIT. Copyright © 2024 by Adam Gamal.
All rights reserved. Printed in the United States of America. For information,
address St. Martin's Publishing Group, 120 Broadway, New York, NY 10271.

www.stmartins.com

Library of Congress Cataloging-in-Publication Data

Names: Gamal, Adam, author. | Kennedy, Kelly, author.
Title: The Unit : my life fighting terrorists as one of America's most secret
    military operatives / Adam Gamal ; with Kelly Kennedy.
Other titles: My life fighting terrorists as one of America's most secret
    military operatives
Description: First edition. | New York : St. Martin's Press, 2024. |
    Includes bibliographical references and index.
Identifiers: LCCN 2023036067 | ISBN 9781250278173 (hardcover) |
    ISBN 9781250278180 (ebook)
Subjects: LCSH: Gamal, Adam. | United States. Army. Special Forces—
    Biography. | United States. Army—Commando troops. | Special
    operations (Military science)—United States—History. | Terrorism—
    Prevention—United States. | Egyptian Americans—Biography. |
    Muslims—United States—Biography.
Classification: LCC UA34.S64 G36 2024 | DDC 356.1670973 [B]—dc23/
    eng/20230112
LC record available at https://lccn.loc.gov/2023036067

Our books may be purchased in bulk for promotional, educational,
or business use. Please contact your local bookseller or the Macmillan Corporate
and Premium Sales Department at 1-800-221-7945, extension 5442, or by email
at MacmillanSpecialMarkets@macmillan.com.

First Edition: 2024

10 9 8 7 6 5 4 3 2 1

Without the foundation my parents set for me, I would never have made it anywhere. However, without the support, encouragement, and wisdom of my wife, I would have been dead by now. And without seeing the hope in my daughters' eyes, I would have never gone the extra mile.

To the souls of my parents, and to my lovely wife.

To my adorable daughters: Do not let anyone slow you down.

And a very special thanks to my great coauthor Kelly Kennedy. I could not have done it without your talent, patience, and dedication to this book.

CONTENTS

CONTENTS

THE UNIT

AUTHOR'S NOTE

WHEN I LANDED IN the United States at the age of twenty on a shiny day in July 1991, I felt as if I could breathe for the first time.

In Egypt, where I was born, I did not have the freedom to breathe deeply, dream big, or jump high. As I grew, Egypt recovered—from a coup that had taken place four decades prior but still affected our daily life. To live in Egypt was to search constantly for a sense of self, to the extent that the late President Anwar Sadat called his book *In Search of Identity*. Most Egyptians are not fully Arabs, not fully Africans, and not fully Mediterranean. The military coup of 1952 deprived Egyptians of being just Egyptian. That affected many young men and women, me included.

But on the day I landed in the land of the free, home of the brave, I filled my lungs with clean, crisp air and made a mental note: This is my chosen home. I will never go back.

A year later, I watched a young Bill Clinton debate a wartime president, President George H. W. Bush, whom I admired greatly. I could barely order breakfast, let alone follow the logic of a debate, but I did understand I was watching democracy in action: Americans not afraid to talk about how they would make their country better, even in the presence of a sitting leader. That debate made me all the more determined to be an American, as well as to serve in the military.

Nearly thirty years later, I see a different America. I see an America unwilling to open its arms to welcome newcomers. As an immigrant, I served in the military for more than twenty years. I fought, I bled, and I almost died to make sure others would have the same opportunities I had—and, if I did it right, even more opportunities. From the snow of Bosnia to the deserts of Iraq, from the hills of Yemen to the mountains of Africa, I fought in every war since 1995. I deployed more than fourteen times to make sure all Americans feel safe and are also treated fairly and equally. We Americans believe everyone has a right to food, shelter, safety, and a sense of belonging—even the pursuit of happiness. But now, many great Americans lack that sense of belonging because of their religion, their national origin, or the color of their skin. I know that's not America. Most Americans are kind, welcoming, and helpful—take it from an immigrant who couldn't find his way out of a New York train station on his first day here.

So let me tell you a story: It's a story of action and adventure, of sorrow and loss, of love and citizenship, of pride and acceptance.

It's a story of a battle against an enemy that began in my youth and continues even now—with ideas about a way forward for my new nation. It's a story of building the American Dream, and always, it is a story of hope.

My disclaimer:

As you read this, there are many great Americans who continue to take the fight to the enemy. Therefore, I initially used only first names or pseudonyms. I sought approval from people whose true first name I am using. I am not disclosing any true locations, mission specifics, means or methods, or anything that might jeopardize the security of my fellow Americans. For the safety of my family and my teammates, I am also not using my true name. While all my teammates can tell who wrote this book, I know none of them would disclose any true names, for our safety and the safety of our families.

This book has gone through prepublication review by the Unit and Pentagon officials, and they determined that I should call this book *The Unit* rather than the nickname I originally planned to use. You'll find the blacked-out copy—the redactions—from that process on some pages.

I am not writing this book for fame or money but rather to tell the story of some of America's finest—the unsung heroes Americans should know about. Heroes come in all colors and shapes, as well as with differing religious beliefs and traditions—including Islam and Judaism. Most Americans expect military heroes to look like Tom Hanks in *Saving Private Ryan*, but I am here to prove some true soldiers look nothing like that.

I plan to contribute some of the proceeds from this book to

support veterans, Gold Star families, and immigrants in need. This book is for veterans and immigrants alike.

DoD Disclaimer:

The views expressed in this publication are those of the author and do not necessarily reflect the official policy or position of the Department of Defense or the US government. The public release clearance of this publication by the Department of Defense does not imply Department of Defense endorsement or factual accuracy of the material.

ONE ONE CRAZY EGYPTIAN

A US NAVY SHIP sits off the Horn of Africa with $5 million worth of missiles waiting for confirmation from a guy—me— who grew up selling vegetables on the streets of Alexandria, Egypt.

I have until five minutes before the missiles hit to divert them. They are aimed at the house of the leader of the Somali branch of al-Qaeda. He's exactly what you'd expect him to be: a tyrant and a big fish in a small town. Each bloody bit of proof of his worth to senior national al-Qaeda leadership grows increasingly violent. Tortured nuns. Executed nurses. A dead reporter.

The attempted demise of my second kidney.

Aden Hashi Ayro is young and short with a small frame, like me, but after training in Afghanistan with al-Qaeda long before

1

the attacks of September 11, 2001, he returned to Africa with Mujahideen street cred. He is believed to have killed BBC journalist Kate Peyton, and he led Hizbul Shabaab—the terrorist organization that seized control of much of Somalia, including Mogadishu, in 2006—as well as al-Qaeda in Somalia.

In 2005, he threw hundreds of corpses from an Italian cemetery in Mogadishu into the sea and then built a mosque in the cemetery's place. He used it to train men in his image.

Not the Islam my father taught me.

It's now 2008. We've searched for him for four years. Each time my team gets eyes on, he slips away.

Every damned time, we lose Ayro at the last minute, so we can't call the air strike.

We have preapproval to call in the strikes. When we have a fixed location on Ayro, we watch him. Eyes on, every day, for more than a week.

And he disappears.

Fucker. He's either really smart or one lucky son of a bitch.

Like so many times in the past, we've lost him twice this week.

The task force commander calls me and says one of our air assets has been pulled away. He says we should just pack it up.

"Let's give it one more day," I say. "I got a gut feeling we'll do it tonight."

Just as we're ready to give up, we get another lead. This time, we know Ayro's ▮▮▮▮▮. We confirm his location on the basis of new information. We know where he is. We know how to limit the civilian casualties.

Eyes on. We got him.

We receive word that there's a mosque at the compound where he's staying. If there's a mosque, there's no missile strike.

"No, no," I tell the team, "that's not how it works. It's a room where he prays. Everyone has a room with a prayer rug."

Even I, on this mission, have a room with a prayer rug. My room. We're golden. We're finally going to get this guy.

Another trip to Somalia, and then, by 3:00 a.m., we've got everything set up.

It's May. Hot, humid, even in the middle of the night. Sweat, gritty from unpaved roads, beads my face and that of the fellow operative, Eddie, who I've brought for his crazy computer skills.

"Hey, man," Eddie says as we prepare. "How does my hair look?"

"Who the fuck cares about your hair?" I say, laughing for the only time that night. He's consistent. Dependable. Funny.

And suave.

Latino and smallish, he could pass for another Arab.

Eddie and I see scenery similar to that of *Black Hawk Down*, and I'd be lying if I said we didn't picture Chief Warrant Officer Mike Durant being dragged naked through the streets of Mogadishu in 1993. That's the horror story every soldier works to avoid: no man left behind.

I fumble with the radio. We've got eyes on. We've had him at the same place long enough, which we relay to our task force commander.

This is what we do. We provide the intelligence that allows other Special Forces operators to go in and execute the target. ███████████████████ we also know how to win hearts and minds to gain information.

We're just quiet about it.

Gray.

For now, it's only Eddie and me.

I start emailing the task force commander, who's a Navy SEAL. A few years after this mission, he will become a SEAL Team commander.

"I trust you," he tells me. "Do what you have to do, but stay safe. Keep staying safe."

We're going to get him. Tonight feels different.

And also the same.

We know nothing good will happen if we are discovered playing with a radio in the middle of the night. And this time, we're on our own. I've heard it straight from the task force commander's mouth.

We're careful. Silent. We sit in darkness.

I cannot fuck this up.

Ayro represents exactly the reason I chose Africa over Iraq or Afghanistan as my mission focus: In Iraq and Afghanistan, the militants appear fully hatched—ready to blow themselves up to spread their toxic ideology in a spray of blood and gristle. Too far gone. But first they come to Africa to learn the trade, to swallow a false doctrine whole—like teenage cult members too bored or lonely to think for themselves. Ayro—and others like him—provide the training and the impetus for blind rage.

Ayro represents the source of the river.

Iraq and Afghanistan sit downstream.

Ayro also represents the men my father protected me from in my childhood: the members of the Muslim Brotherhood in Egypt who saw my success in school and in sports and sought to recruit me to their cause.

Eyes on.

I send the ten-digit grid coordinates. This allows the missiles to hit within one meter of the house. It's basically brick and mud—some of the nearby homes look as if they were built from bales of hay. Some have walls made of corrugated sheet metal. Others have tin roofs.

I think Ayro hides here because it's tiny—about nine thousand people, most of them his clan. Everybody knows everybody, one big family. As a Muslim man, I fit in pretty well. I'm brown. I have the accent. I know which hand to use for a country dinner. But the al-Qaeda guys are slippery.

The stores in Dusa Marreb have their names painted on the front. It would be like if your neighbor walked outside his house and hand-painted "Bob's Restaurant" on the front with maybe a picture of a fish. Except, because Somalia used to be a big area for tourism—the beach in Mogadishu was lined with balconied hotels with arabesque windows, and wildlife parks drew thousands of people before the civil war began in 1991—everybody names their restaurants after the Indian Ocean.

Bob's Indian Ocean Restaurant.

Picture of a fish.

The women wear the abaya—that big black dress that covers everything. Some of them wear black gloves. They all wear headscarves. The men wear something called a *macawis*—it's a man skirt. They look like large handkerchiefs in bright colors that have been tied at the waist. They wear them with short-sleeved, button-down shirts or with T-shirts handed off from other coun-tries: "Just Do Me." "Chicago Bears—Super Bowl Champions 2007." Sparkly pink unicorns.

"Jackpot," I type. "We have eyes on."

Every five minutes, I will verify that Ayro's still here: "Jackpot."

Around me, the darkness of the town highlights the illumi-nated sky—just like what I saw in the countryside as a child: A bright moon, moving slowly. Millions of stars.

"Jackpot," I type. "Still fixed."

We fuss with the equipment, talk about the target. I'm not afraid, exactly. In Islam, we believe that whatever is meant to hap-pen to us will happen. If it's my time, it's out of my hands—not that I want another bullet in the gut.

"Still eyes on," I type.

It will take an hour from the time I type in the coordinates for the missiles to arrive in Dusa Marreb from the middle of the Indian Ocean.

"Jackpot."

We need to get this guy.

By now, the missiles have been in the air for forty-five min-utes. It feels like days. Time goes just as slowly as it did two years before this trip, when I spent time in a dirty hospital recovering from a gunshot wound. One inch to the right, and I would have been paralyzed.

Fuckers.

It will be worth it, I tell myself.

The signal gets weak. I focus on commo gears as Eddie finds a Gatorade bottle we've brought to urinate in and uses it to adjust the angle of the antenna.

"What the fuck, man?" I say. "What if we need to piss?"

"Two is one and one is none," he tells me, showing me a second bottle. Always prepared.

"Jackpot," I relay back to the Task Force Command Team through my commo equipment, which is now jerry-rigged with a piss-bottle antenna. "The target is still there."

"Thank you, Eddie," I say.

"Why are you thanking me, man?" he says. "We are one team, brother."

This is Eddie's first mission in Africa—he'd been based in South America—and he trusts me with his life. I cannot fuck this up.

I cannot get him killed. It would kill me to make that call to his wife. I work to keep us safe. I focus on keeping alive two people who are already ghosts, already off the military rolls because of our work in the Unit, the military's most secret intelligence/special operations unit. We simply do not exist.

"Eyes on," I type.

It's sobering. I don't want to say it's easier to shoot someone face-to-face, but if you're shooting at somebody face-to-face, it's probably because he's shooting at you. You know he's a bad guy. He's showing you he's a bad guy. He has the weapon in his hands. And you have only a split second to fire. Over the course of an hour, I have a lot of time to think about what I'm doing. *Is the right guy there? Who else is there? Are there kids there? Is his wife there? Are there other women in the house?* All of these things go through my mind. I need to be certain. I need to be accurate.

I'm not thinking about whether it's the right thing or not because I already know it's the right thing.

"Still there?"

"Yes. He's still there."

We wait. Eddie and I watch.

Is anyone coming out?

Is anyone going in?

I've got until five minutes before the missiles hit to divert them.

I could send them to a "neutral" zone, allowing sand and brush to absorb the force of three $1.4 million guided bombs.

Still there.

"Let's finish this," I say to Eddie.

Still a go.

"All it takes is one fucking crazy Egyptian," our analyst says.

Correction: one fucking crazy American.

WHEN I WAS SIX and living in Alexandria, I sneaked out of the
house and wandered the two blocks down to the beach. So many
famous eyes had gazed upon the water from that shore: Alexander the Great. Cleopatra. Callimachus. Julius Caesar.

I saw waves and birds, inhaled salt and sea, and I became en-
thralled by the bigness of it all. When my family found me, I was
soaking wet and breathing in great, rasping heaves. I remember my mother throwing my little body over her shoulder and
sprinting to the hospital. It was less than five minutes away, but
as I fought to breathe, it felt like a lifetime. In 1976, the doctors
diagnosed me with a lung condition and said I would be lucky to
live until the age of twelve.

"The doctors said you're not going to live," my mother told me, as if describing the *kushari* she had for lunch. "But you'll be fine."

In some ways, I was too young to care. I just wanted to play.

But a few times a week, my mother rushed me to the hospital for a shot to allow air to fill my lungs. I hated shots. I remember feeling confused and weak but also disgusted by the medicinal smell of the hospital—bleach and blood and vomit. I learned quickly that I did not like to feel helpless.

Just north of the Valley of Kings, I started life as a skinny kid with asthma.

My parents were good to each other—kind and close.

We lived in a two-bedroom apartment, the six of us. My parents took one bedroom, my sisters took one bedroom, and my brother and I slept in the living room. It was small, but it was close to the beach and to the university, the hospitals, and the schools—it was a strategic geographic location, and that's why my dad picked it.

Two bedrooms were all he could afford in that neighborhood. He wanted to raise us in a middle-class neighborhood, rather than a poor neighborhood, because the schools would be better. There were no school buses in Egypt, but Dad picked a place close enough to school that we could walk. When I was little, it was a short walk. In high school, it was about four miles each way, six days a week.

Already, I was being conditioned for long walks.

My mother left school after second grade. Her father did not believe in educating girls. She was determined that we would have that opportunity but also that we would be good humans. If we lied? Ass whooping. Lying did not help us make good decisions. She was the one who assigned the chores: Laundry. Dishes. Taking out the trash.

I was the trash guy. Taking out the trash in Egypt is not like taking out the trash in the United States. I had to walk down the street to the dumpster. I was small, and I had to heave that shit up and over and into a mess of other trash. I made the mistake of not properly tying the bag only once. Picture a dumpster with a neighborhood's trash in 110-degree heat in the middle of the night: Rats. Stench. Roaches.

Mom knew exactly what she was doing.

My dad read everything to compensate for a lack of a formal education. When he arrived in Alexandria from his small farm town, he could hold his own in conversations. He liked to talk about politics, and he wanted to be around people who could talk about what he saw as the important issues. He liked to sit and observe—a trait I inherited. I think it was in his DNA to be kind.

When my dad got to Alexandria, he had no skills—besides farming. He worked in a factory for about a year, but he studied and took a test for a government job. He read enough and worked hard enough that he got a job as a safety technician with the Egyptian Navy.

Still, because he didn't have a degree—because of that piece of paper—he saw that he would never be able to reach his full potential.

"You guys will graduate from college," he used to tell us.

When I walked out my front door, the sun hit me full force, daily: Brown boy, dark mop of hair. City-kid clothes. If I walked left, I saw Roman statues. If I walked right, I could wander through a Roman theater with its Corinthian columns.

Alexandria is not like Cairo with pyramids and Pharaonic and Arabic influences. Alexander the Great built my hometown, so it's a Greek city, originally. Near my house sat the Roman Theatre. Not too far away you'd find the Kom el Shoqafa burial grounds from the second century, which merged Roman, Greek, and Egyptian influences—the Egyptian god of the dead guards the entrance, wearing Roman clothing—into three levels of catacombs. You can see Pompey's Pillar; an ancient Arab wall; the site of the Pharos Lighthouse, where Fort Qaitbey now sits; and the Abu Abbas al-Mursi Mosque, which was built in 1796. Much of the architecture overlooking the beach is European, from the days when England occupied Egypt.

When Malcolm X visited Cairo in the early 1960s, he said it felt more like Europe than the Middle East—it's less like that now, but then it felt like a Mediterranean city. If you asked people their ethnicity, they would say "Mediterranean," "North African," or "Middle Eastern"—rarely would you hear "Arabic." Looking around, that made sense.

In the 1970s, in places like Egypt and Syria and Lebanon, things felt pretty modern—and pretty westernized. The young university women wore miniskirts and bell-bottom pants. They dressed like what we saw on Western TV shows. We shopped at "megastores," which were the equivalent of a shopping mall.

In the port, we saw commercial and naval ships, and in the morning, we watched the fishing boats go out. If we helped the fishermen pull out their nets, they would reward us with free fish at the end of the day.

It was a happy childhood.

Alexandria had European quarters and Greek quarters and

neighborhoods where the Black Africans—many from Sudan—lived (Egyptians are, of course, also African). There were immigrants from Mediterranean countries: A certain class of people spoke French. Our grocery store was run by a Greek Christian guy. He sold beer. But he wouldn't let us buy it from him, because he knew our families. He taught us integrity. The tailor was Italian. Our barber was European of some variety. Another neighbor owned a garage. If he saw us joking around not doing anything, he'd say, "Come and help me wipe down this car." If my Boy Scout uniform didn't look right, someone would stop me: "Let me help you with your shirt." I had Christian friends growing up. I learned to pick my friends for how they treated me.

Even within my family, there are differences: I have blond cousins. My brother looks like a white dude. I'm the darkest one in my family. Ultimately, everybody was just Alexandrian.

In Egypt every spring, we celebrated Sham El-Nessim, which means "inhaling the breeze." It's everything springtime and is similar to Easter, but it goes back to the time of the Pharaohs. In ancient times, the festival began when the sun aligned with the Great Pyramid of Giza. The ancients colored eggs, then wrote wishes on them and hung them on trees, hoping that the gods would see them. Old-school shit. When I was a kid, every year, a parade with Mickey Mouse and the Easter Bunny would wend its way through the city. New-school shit.

(And fun.)

The ancient sea breeze continued to call me: Inhale. Two years after my asthma attack, I started running the same beach that had almost killed me to "put muscle on my legs." I always appeared much younger than I was, and bullies looking for the littlest kid may have inspired my need for strength. Every year—every single year—at the beginning of the year, someone would try to bully me, and I would fight back.

My mother pushed me toward sports. She worried about my lungs, my stature, those bullies. To compensate, I needed to run fast, to be strong.

That same year, when I was eight, I started to play basketball. I used to measure how high I could jump—and compete with my brother. We tried to touch the ceiling. I jumped until I could reach the basketball net.

But I also worked on my mind: I started to play chess that year, too—maybe I could outsmart the bullies. I became the best player in the district. Academically, I was in the top of my class.

My parents encouraged my efforts, my mother by acting as if what the doctors said was complete nonsense and treating me exactly like the other children, and my father by acting as a shadow throughout my youth.

During Ramadan, we fasted the whole month during the day, starting that same year when I was eight, and it would be so hot—no water until evening. My mom used to soak me down with a hose.

"You're just little," she would say. "It's okay for you to have a little water."

But I was stubborn.

Preparation.

Ramadan is always in the ninth month of the Islamic calendar, and fasting is one of the five pillars in Islam, which are the things you are meant to do as a good Muslim. (The others are declaring one's faith in God, daily prayer, giving alms, and a pilgrimage to

Mecca.) It's similar to giving up something for Lent—fasting is a path toward spiritual growth through physical means. During Ramadan, Muslims don't eat, drink (even water), or have sexual relations from sunrise until sunset every day. Some people pray more, too. And then we celebrate, because Muslims believe that God revealed the Quran to the Prophet Muhammad during the last ten days of Ramadan.

The whole neighborhood got involved, no matter whether they were Muslim or not—it's like Christmas in the United States, home of the Hanukkah bush. Even atheists love Santa. In a hot country, we had small ovens in our homes, but everyone baked huge numbers of pastries and cookies for Ramadan. My brother and I would go to the local bakery and rent a baking sheet, then my mother would fill it with different kinds of sweets. She'd write our name on it, and then my brother and I would go stand in line with all the other families with their trays and chitchat and joke. It was festive. The Christian families would do the same thing—it was fun. There just wasn't that division.

At least, that's how I remember it.

At night, after we had broken our fast, my friends and I would walk the streets of Alexandria until the early hours of the morning, gazing at so many tiny twinkling lights strung across millennia-old roads from centuries-old buildings—mosques and Roman pillars and shops—that it felt as if we traveled through a cocoon of bright stars and crescents.

People hung tin lanterns with intricate patterns and colorful paper lanterns from their balconies. Ornaments, similar to Christmas ornaments, hung from every available space. In Egypt, we love brightly colored wall hangings with bits of mirror woven in, and the glass shapes reflected the light. It was magic—like a fairyland. Public Iftar tables—where people broke the fast each evening for a month—lined the streets and seemed as if they went on for miles.

We ate *konafa*, a thread-thin shredded pastry layered with a cream or nuts-and-raisins filling and then soaked in syrup.

It felt like a carnival.

We played soccer on streets that had been blocked for the festivities, and we felt safe and loved by all the neighbors we saw gathered to celebrate the "month of great blessings."

My Egypt was not the Sphinx surrounded by pyramids and desert. Every summer, we went to my grandparents' farms. As we drove south into the center of the Nile delta from Alexandria, we saw green in every direction—a land of fertility.

About an hour south of Alexandria, there's a town called Damanhur. From there, we took a dirt road for about another half an hour to my father's parents' house.

As we came into town—just before a canal where I almost drowned—one of my paternal grandfather's dogs would meet us. He'd run alongside the car, wriggling his tail and happy, and that would mark the beginning of summer.

My maternal uncle, my other grandfather's chosen heir to his land, would sometimes meet us with his tractor. He was kind and fun and huge. He had six fingers on one hand, and the family said, "God knew he was going to be a hard worker, so he gave him some extra help." On the tractor, my mom would take the only other seat, but my uncle's shoulders were so wide that my brother and sisters and I would simply cling to him. My sisters sat in his lap. I'd saddle my tiny legs around his neck and grip his forehead.

Air that smelled like grass. People who loved us. The scent of the Nile, which had nurtured millions before us. No brick walls covering our windows to protect us from war, as they did in Alexandria.

Summer.

We thought we went for fun—a vacation—but really we went so my dad could save money: at the farm, he didn't have to feed us. Dad would hire a car, and my brother, sisters, mom, and I would load up and head out with all our suitcases. My dad would then head back to Alexandria to work, while we spent the summer in the country. We loved it because we could play and run around with bare feet.

My grandfather—my father's father—built a big house with several apartments for his sons and their families, and he had farms spread throughout the area. He rotated his crops: cotton, pears, corn, tomatoes, cucumbers.

At night, we'd go out into the fields and build a bonfire and roast the corn. We'd eat it with cucumbers and tomatoes my grandfather had grown.

Most homes in the area didn't have phones or electricity, and if they had electricity, it didn't always work. No television. I'd wake with the sun, as early as 5:00 a.m., and I played with my cousins. I had more than twenty of them, and they were creative. We didn't have fishing poles, so we punched holes in big trays and scooped the trays through the water to catch fish. My grandmother loved us, but she didn't love what we did to her pots and pans.

Preparation.

I learned a lot during that time—it made me tough. I could walk with no shoes. I, just like the Nebraska farm kids who joined me in selection, could play in the sun all day without drinking water or eating. I was being prepared for my unit's selection without knowing.

There was no such thing as air-conditioning or "too hot, so I'm not going to do it." We worked hard.

By the time I got to the military, that stuff was easy.

I had other preparation: every summer, I would have an accident. One time, as a ragtag group of us rode a tractor, I hung off the back. Somebody pushed me—playing around and trying to take my spot—and I fell, and the tractor ran over my foot. Everybody ran to tell my mother.

"Hey! Your son just died!"

I didn't die.

But I couldn't walk for the rest of the summer. They put my foot in a cast, and I wasn't allowed to put any weight on it for two months.

Another time, I fell in a canal used for collecting the village sewage. As I played with a cousin, I simply slipped off the edge. One of my female cousins cleaned me up before I went back to the house—I smelled like shit—so I wouldn't be punished. Years later, the swimming portion of selection proved to be the hardest part for me mentally. As I treaded water and dove for weights wearing all of my clothing—boots, too—and gear, all I could think about was that dark, diseased water filling my lungs, as well as the seaside adventure that left me weak as a child. But that near drowning in the canal likely hardened me, even if it left me with a fear of water.

I'm not fond of shit, either.

Resilient. I did not fear pain or risk. Perhaps I was already addicted to adrenaline.

Or perhaps I was just clumsy.

In the countryside, my cousins looked out for me—when they weren't teasing me themselves.

In the Army, if I talked about those days, a pal would tell a similar story about a farm in the States—whether we were kids in the valleys of Egypt or the plains of the Midwest, we played the same games and learned the same lessons. (I may have been the only one who fell off a camel.) But those similarities help free us from our preconceived ideas about people.

At the farm, if we weren't playing, our uncles grilled us. They expected us to know moderate Islam—and math. We faced math drills from relatives at any moment.

"If you left Alexandria at 10:00 a.m. going ninety miles per hour to Cairo, what time would you meet your brother coming from Alexandria at 10:30 a.m. going eighty miles per hour?" my uncle would ask.

Just when we thought we'd recovered from that, we'd get, "What's 743 times 64?" and we'd grab a pencil. "No, do it in your head."

None of these guys had more than a high school education, but they were brilliant.

My father would hit us with riddles.

"What is the creature that walks on four legs in the morning, two legs at noon, and three in the evening?"

The riddle of the Sphinx. The riddle of man.

That's how they taught us.

My paternal grandfather was the mayor of his village. To get into the university, my grandfather would have memorized the entire Quran by heart before he was fifteen.

Then he taught it to my father and to my uncles.

He taught them moderate Islam.

"What these other people are talking about is not Islam," he told them.

Aden Ayro would not have impressed my grandfather.

My mom's father was a self-made man, and he was wealthier than my other grandfather. He was a man of few words, but we saw him as kinder than my other grandfather, who lived about half an hour away. My mom's father would wake up at four or five—before morning prayer—and ride his horse around his property. He had a lot of orchards, and people used to take the fruit from his trees. A couple of pieces of fruit is okay, but people would take a lot. So, some mornings, he would fire a couple of rounds from his old Russian-made rifle into the air, and then he would go to *fajr*—the first prayer of the day—at the mosque.

"Hey," people would say when he arrived. "We heard gunfire from your property this morning."

"Yes," he would say. "There were foxes."

Red foxes. Gray foxes were not yet native to Egypt.

Because people were afraid of the foxes, they avoided his property. Of course, there were no foxes, but he was a sneaky old wise man. He spent time learning about his adversaries, building relationships, and studying situations until he found the best solution.

I learned from him, too.

WHEN WE WENT BACK home at the end of the sunny summer, darkness filled our apartment during the day. All of the apartment buildings in Alexandria had brick walls in front of them to block bombs and shrapnel. But the walls also prevented the sunlight from coming in through the windows—especially in a ground-floor apartment.

When I was small, Egypt was at war with Israel. US troops still deploy to the Sinai Desert, home of the Suez Canal, to maintain the peace brokered when I was in grade school.

It's funny to think about now, but one of my favorite childhood memories is political. In 1978, President Jimmy Carter visited Egypt, and my dad and I watched excitedly as he drove past in a convertible Cadillac with President Anwar Sadat. As an eight-year-old kid, I thought, *This is the coolest thing ever*. Sadat had signed a peace treaty with Israel, with the help of Carter, after leading Egypt in the Yom Kippur War. So, in Egypt, we called Sadat the "president of war and peace." I think of the guy as a visionary—people still celebrate that there's been forty years of peace because of Sadat.

Soon after Carter visited, Egypt and Israel began their peace talks. Then the Egyptian government began to take down the brick walls in front of our homes—I remember that vividly. Light suddenly filled our apartment, and that brightness corresponds in my mind with the peace celebrations. It was like living in a new world.

But as a kid, I didn't see or understand the other changes—the walls that went up to replace those that had once guarded our apartment. They came gradually, almost imperceptibly.

We watched news of the war in Afghanistan on TV. Egypt wanted US support because they wanted US money, so they sent kids there to fight with the Mujahideen against the Russians. But then they came back with new ideas from the extremists. The speeches in the mosques and the preaching changed.

Sadat was my hero, but he played a game with religion, and it bit him, and Egypt, in the ass. In the name of religious freedom, or to counter the socialists left over from the Gamal Abdel Nasser regime, he allowed the Muslim Brotherhood to have a bigger voice, and they grew more influential. They pretend to be peaceful, but ultimately, they are extremist Muslims who want a strict, conservative state where everyone must obey their rules.

Women started to cover up. Men started to grow beards and wear the *jalabiya* thing—we had only seen farmers wear the

ankle-length white shift before, and even that was rare. Aden
Ayro could trace his roots to this cultural change.

After militants assassinated Sadat, President Hosni Mubarak
continued to give the Brotherhood "controlled" power. He
worked for peace by allowing everyone—including the Muslim
Brotherhood—to have a seat at the table, even though he knew how
corrupt the Brotherhood is.

In fact, he allowed every clown to talk as long as they didn't
do anything too crazy. Obviously, I am not against freedom of
speech, but I am against irresponsible speeches that incite vio-
lence, especially when religion is used, which ultimately can kill
the voice of reason. Mubarak would pay for that later. He arrested
some members of the Muslim Brotherhood, including the guys
who killed Sadat, but he allowed a lot of other guys to talk, including the Blind Sheikh, Omar Abdel-Rahman. The Blind Sheikh
was prosecuted for Sadat's death because he issued a fatwa calling for it.

I'll tell you more about him later because I kept running into
that fucker. He had childhood diabetes, which left him blind, so
he studied the Quran in braille. A regular Helen Keller.

He spent three years in jail after Sadat's death. He led an organization called the Islamic Group (al-Jama'a al-Islamiyya). I hated
those guys.

All of a sudden, everything was haram. Forbidden. Aden
Ayro's Islam.

Bunch of angry mofos.

In the meantime, the oil industry started to boom in Saudi
Arabia, so Egyptians traveled there to work as teachers and
doctors—and in the oil fields. At the time, we saw Saudi Arabia

as synonymous with Islam. Mecca. We face there when we pray. But the people who went to work in Saudi Arabia came home with a different version of Islam.

Mubarak created an opening. He allowed all kinds of mosques, so anyone could start one and preach whatever they wanted to preach. The extremists were also allowed to go to Afghanistan to fight against the former Soviet Union, so they came back even more extreme. Many mosques became militarized.

We heard on the radio that the young Egyptian men fighting in Afghanistan were killing the infidels.

Street imams. They read a couple of books, and, suddenly, they reemerged as spiritual leaders. They said that when the Mujahideen died in Afghanistan, the people around them smelled roses—the sweet smell of heaven. Bullshit. I've been around when the so-called Mujahideen die in Afghanistan, and it smells an awful lot like somebody just died—same as anyone else.

Wagdy Abd el-Hamied Mohamed Ghoneim's voice filled my head—not intentionally. He was a Salafi Muslim imam from Alexandria, and he preached hatred, recording his messages on cassette tapes. He was background noise in the streets.

The tapes were ubiquitous: We heard them being played in cars as they drove past on the street. We heard them on boom boxes. We heard them in our playmates' homes. "Let me read you a letter from a fighter." "God is protecting the Mujahideen." "A Muslim fighter closed his eyes and fired, and he hit a truck filled with Soviet ammo, and it killed all of the Soviet fighters. God is great."

I imagine those guys do, in fact, have better luck with their aim when they close their eyes.

"Two weeks after our fighter died, when they went to bury him, his body was intact, and he had a smile on his face. He is a martyr."

It sounded as if these guys didn't really die: they just took a nap.

Always curious, I listened. If my father found Ghoneim's tapes, he threw them in the trash. "Don't listen to that."

But the government condoned it simply by allowing Ghoneim to spew his bullshit.

Secretively, the Muslim Brotherhood told young kids like me that art in school was haram. Singing was haram. Dancing was haram. They were allowed to quietly make everything haram. Sound familiar? Organizations like the Taliban, al-Shabaab, and ISIS still follow the teachings of the Muslim Brotherhood.

It was like a government-sanctioned mass brainwashing, but I could never tell if it was because the government was too ignorant to see it or because they simply ignored it. But how do you, as the government, ignore that these guys say the national anthem is haram?

As a ten-year-old kid? We took it all in. Indoctrination.

It was funny: We lived between the beach and the tram, so I felt as if I could go anywhere. There were movie theaters nearby where you could buy popcorn and see the world in a different way, but there were also a lot of mosques. Alexandria's not the capital, so while it's a large city, there isn't a heavy government influence there.

That made it a good place for the Muslim Brotherhood to recruit and be based.

Russia eventually deserted Afghanistan—fled—in 1989. Russia, the United States, Pakistan, Egypt, and Saudi Arabia let Afghanistan collapse, and they failed the Afghan people. The Muslim extremists spawned during my childhood in Egypt by the Muslim Brotherhood arrived in Afghanistan in full force, offering food and jobs and medicine and "education"—brainwashing in the guise of religion and hope. The government let the genie out of the bottle, and this wasn't the Disney version.

Dad worried that I would befriend the wrong people, develop hateful ideas.

He watched me play sports. My dad would walk into my school like it was the most normal thing in the world to interrupt the teacher in the classroom.

"Hey," he'd say. "I'm his father. How's he doing?"

The teacher would fill him in. I mean, I was making good grades and excelling in sports. I was doing just fine. But that wasn't it, really. He wanted me—and anyone who might try to interfere with what he taught me at home—to know he was paying attention.

"By the way," he'd say to the teacher, "if he misbehaves, you have permission to spank him."

In front of my classmates. I'd try to sink underneath my desk. Dad even inspired prayer: "God, please don't let him come to school again."

When I was in fifth grade, my teacher asked me to bring my dad in. I told my dad, and I immediately got the hard stare—the "What did you do wrong?" stare. My teacher would say only that it was something good. Dad went in, and she told him I was advanced for my class and she'd like for me to skip a year and go straight to sixth grade, which is middle school in Egypt. She said

I was going to be bored in fifth grade. "He's way ahead of them," she told him.

My father looked at her, and then he looked at the rest of the kids in the class. She told him all of this in front of me. He pulled her aside and talked to her for a bit. And then he left. But I was in fifth grade, so nobody told me anything.

"What happened?" I asked when I got home.

"I'm not going to let you skip a year," he said.

"Why?" I asked. I wanted to be in the class ahead of me.

"You're already the smallest kid in the class," he said. "In the next class up, you'll be that much smaller than the smallest kid. And you'd be the youngest. So no."

When I was in high school in Egypt, the government decided several schools should be military schools. In each district, they picked the best school, and it became a military school. They chose my school. Of course, we had to wear a uniform. Blue pants, blue shirt, navy-blue sweater, and black shoes.

It had to be black shoes.

I didn't have black shoes, and my parents didn't have the money to buy me black shoes. So I wore brown shoes.

Every morning, we had formations. If we were out of uniform in the formation, we would be punished. Every day, I showed up in my brown shoes. And every day, the military officer in charge of the formation would come and find me in my brown shoes. Every day, he would punish me by making me stand at the position of attention for an hour.

Finally, in formation one day, I said, "I'm not wearing brown shoes because I'm disrespectful. I'm wearing brown shoes because

I don't own black shoes." The guy felt bad about it, but he told me I had to follow the rules. And he kept punishing me.

The rules don't change because you're poor.

Yes, there are several directions you can go with that: Give the kids with brown shoes black shoes. Change the rules so that brown shoes or black shoes are just fine, as long as they have been polished. Give the kid with brown shoes a deadline to come up with a pair of black shoes. But the reality is that most people, especially in situations that are authoritarian by nature, aren't that creative. I, as a teenager, had to be. I saw it as a challenge, and I used it to grow stronger.

By the time I graduated, I could stand at the position of attention for days—and I could do it without thinking too much about the fairness of being punished for being poor.

But even school felt like a place that had to be navigated to avoid extremists. I remember singing the Egyptian national anthem one day in school.

"You shouldn't do that," the kid next to me said. "It's haram."

Forbidden.

Preparation.

I went to Boy Scouts (I eventually became an Eagle Scout) at the nearest mosque, and that's where I played basketball and other sports. There was a much older guy whom we looked up to, and he used to bring three of us to the mosque to talk—eight-year-old kids. They started us young, but Dad watched everything.

Dad was always after me: Which mosque are you going to? Who are you going with? Are you staying between prayer times? You'd think my dad would want us to spend as much time as possible at the mosque. Nope. About forty-five minutes separated the last two prayers of the day—the sunset prayer and the evening prayer—so a lot of people just stayed at the mosque. But there was nothing to do there. People socialized or went home and watched one of the two television channels.

There's no denying the militants were smart: they started using that time for lectures. Sometimes those lectures were on the "You've got to prepare for the war against Christians/Jews/Shia/whoever-the-enemy-was-that-day" list, and my dad wasn't having it.

"If you're going to pray," he said, "pray and come back. Don't stay at the mosque."

One day, he was home when the older guy stopped by the house to walk with me to the mosque.

"My son is not going with you anymore," my dad said. No extremists.

Eventually, he asked me to stop going to that mosque.

I made that sound like a request: my dad wasn't messing around.

When we walked together, he would point out the extreme mosques, as well as the mosques where it was safe for me to go.

"We want you to learn discipline," he told me. "You won't eat when it's time to fast. You will give charity to poor people, even if you are poorer than they are. And when you give charity, don't ask what religion the person is. When you're giving charity, it doesn't matter if they're Muslim or Christian."

Dad had us memorize a verse from the Quran:

Goodness does not consist in turning your face towards
East or West. The truly good are those who believe in

God and the Last Day, in the angels, the Scripture, and
the prophets; who give away some of their wealth, how-
ever much they cherish it, to their relatives, to orphans,
the needy, travelers and beggars and to liberate those in
debt and bondage; those who keep up the prayers and
pay the prescribed alms; who keep pledges whenever they
make them; who are steadfast in misfortune, adversity
and times of danger. These are the ones who are true,
and it is they who are aware of God. (Al Quran 2:178)

Dad said it was easy to be a good Muslim: just be a good human being.

And he knew his lessons would have to continue long after he was gone, even if he didn't understand that his teachings would lead me to fight the same enemy he had steered me away from as a child. Aden Ayro was an insult to everything my father taught.

Dad tried to prepare me, to open my mind. He knew that the lessons I learned listening to the radio and talking with people in certain mosques would be hard to defeat: "Islam is the one true religion. Jews are the enemy. There is no reason for any Christian to help a Muslim."

Later I would realize that I had some unlearning to do—that my feelings about Jews and others of any kind weren't as open-minded as my father would have liked, that a friendly neighbor who helped me with my Boy Scout uniform was different in my developing brain from a people as a whole, and that it would take time to truly understand what "not my Islam" meant.

But the lessons did stick, ultimately. It's rare that there isn't an early memory to correspond with what I did later in life: Sayings.

Memorized verses. Hugs after I'd done something well. Even my own anger when I didn't understand something at the time.

When I was fourteen, I started my first job, selling garlic. My dad let me, though he worried that it would interfere with school—but he made me give half of my earnings to my brother because families share. It seemed horribly unfair. Picture a skinny kid in a busy market with a pushcart, negotiating the price of garlic with old people: "Garlic! Get your garlic here!"

The paycheck? Exactly what you would have expected.

"You're going to work hard in your life, either at the beginning or at the end," my father said. "At the end, you may not have as much energy as you do at the beginning, so you may as well get it in now."

It paid off. All four of us have college degrees.

By the time I graduated from high school, I was the best athlete in my class, as well as the top student. I was ready for law school, but I had some work to do before I would be ready to live a life I couldn't begin to imagine.

I was competitive in aggressive ways, and, in my mind, I always track it back to that day at the beach when the doctors told my parents I would fail in life—fail to live.

But I went to the beach because I was curious about the world.

That curiosity would lead me to more than sixty countries before my fortieth birthday.

It would also take me to the most secretive unit in the United States military.

IN 1980, WHEN I was nine—about two years after I began running on the beach and lifting weights—the brand-new Field Operations Group (FOG) sat in a desert in my country preparing a second attempt to save fifty-two American hostages held in Beirut.[1] The first attempt, known as Operation Eagle Claw, failed because the American alphabet agencies couldn't play well together, the CIA refused to share information with the Army's Special Forces units, and field commanders advised President Carter to abort the mission after three of eight military helicopters became dysfunctional—though the mission required only four helicopters to complete. As they

[1]

withdrew from the mission, one of the helicopters crashed into a transport aircraft, killing eight service members. An Iranian civilian was also killed.

My understanding is that the FOG mission, Operation Credible Sport, was successful from an intelligence standpoint, but the Unit couldn't get the military support it needed to carry out the rescue. The hostages remained prisoners for 444 days. ████

██

████████████████████████ During World War II, Office of Strategic Services teams parachuted into France to help organize the resistance during the D-Day landings.[2] And during the Vietnam War, a unit called the Studies and Operations Group (SOG) sought information about the Viet Cong, as well as carrying out psychological warfare.[3]

Each version struggled as Big Army felt the intelligence units imposed upon its territory, and the old-school generals sabotaged operations even as other leaders, including President Kennedy, saw the SOG as the future.

As the FOG worked to find the hostages, the military stood up the Joint Special Operations Command (JSOC). ████████

██

██

██

Because of the FOG's success, the Unit grew and became known as the ███████████████████—or "the Unit." Since I am not allowed to talk about the actual name of the organi-

2 ████████████
3 ████████████

zation, it will be referred to as "the Unit" going forward. ███

███████████████████████████████████ In the beginning, the Unit supported special operations by ████████████

███

███

███

█████████

Over the years, the Unit has faced threats of disbandment, en-
gagement requirements so heavy that they rendered it inactive,
and sudden realizations of its necessity. Ultimately, the group
formed one of America's strongest military units in modern
history—lethal yet under extreme cover.

Early on, the team developed its motto, Send Me, which represents a Bible verse: "Also I heard the voice of the Lord, saying,
'Whom shall I send, and who will go for us?' Then said I, 'Here
am I; send me.'"[4]

As time went on, the Unit's own operatives directly partici-
pated in missions rather than simply providing intelligence. The
team has been involved in everything from finding kidnapped
generals to ensuring that US embassies were safe and rescuing
hostages taken by hijackers. They've been everywhere from Nigeria to El Salvador. They found Pablo Escobar[5] and helped to
capture Radovan Karadžić, the former Bosnian Serb leader.[6]

---

4 ████████████

5 Michael Smith, *Killer Elite: The Inside Story of America's Most Secret Special Operations Team* (New
York: St. Martin's Press, 2007), 190.

6 Smith, 192.

Its members are selected on the basis of their talents, and, from the beginning, the team realized women also had talent—as did people who spoke foreign languages and, at least in the beginning, looked as if they belonged in South America, Southeast Asia, or the Middle East.[7] All of its records are classified, as are its name and location. Each time the Unit's name has become known, the Unit has created a new secret codename.[8]

The current name is classified, and I would give my life to protect the people in it, which means that names in this book have been changed, as have some details to protect my brothers and sisters.

At first, the Unit conducted an awful lot of technical surveillance. They determined where people were on the basis of where line-of-sight and line-of-bearing signals originated. Those methods have become obsolete, and operatives now use new techniques. ███████████████████████████████████
███
███████████

I'm not telling you anything you can't find on the internet or in one of a couple of books about the organization. But I will not confirm the accuracy or—as is much more often the case—inaccuracy of that information.

But I will tell you that, in 1981, the Unit began recruiting operatives.

I am the first of those operatives to tell his story.

---

7 Smith, 29.
8 ███████████

I ARRIVED AT LAW school in Alexandria with not a small amount of awe. It overlooked the same shore that had first inspired my quest for knowledge, and I loved its palm trees and peach-colored buildings—one with a pyramid facade. I loved the dark wood meant to evoke a courtroom, and I loved the hard benches where we sat as wizened professors lectured from behind grand desks on a stage at the front of the room. While my university didn't have the ancient credentials of my grandfather's college, it had created its share of brilliant people, and I had worked hard to get there.

Arrived, I thought. I dreamed of making change, of pushing for an Egypt more like my father's.

In Egypt, as in Europe, I didn't need a four-year degree to go to law school. Instead, directly after high school, I went to law school. Pretty quickly, I realized that the laws I studied did not correlate with the realities of Egypt.

"What you're learning here, you will likely never practice," one of my much-older professors told me. He had been a minister, and he had earned his doctorate in France. He knew what liberty was. He knew what justice was. I believed him.

There would be no justice. I studied law, but there were no human rights in Egypt—no real legal system, no freedom, no possibility of change, and no opportunity at all. Even my right to dream disappeared in law school.

And I still couldn't shake the Muslim Brotherhood.

Just as in my childhood, my abilities attracted them: I was outgoing and social, and I loved to plan activities with my friends.

Ideologically? They didn't care about that.

While I was a freshman, the Muslim Brotherhood asked me to run on their behalf for student government.

Their request astonished me: it's not as if I had been hanging out with them.

"I have nothing to do with you guys," I said. "In fact, I'm the opposite of you."

I told them that even if I did run in their name, I wouldn't represent them, because I liked to hang out in groups of men and women, I didn't believe in their ideology, I liked to think for myself, and I liked to party like any young adult.

"Oh, that's cool," they said. "We just want to maintain the seat."

No thanks.

But they got me thinking. I tend to be competitive, so I went ahead and ran for that seat—against the Muslim Brotherhood candidate.

They were so well organized. They understood grassroots campaigning even before President Barack Obama did. They canvassed door to door on campus, and they had some funding coming to them from somewhere—extremist groups, possibly unofficially sanctioned by the government—so they were even able to do some professional campaigning.

But to the surprise of everyone, including me, I won.

I didn't go out of my way to irritate them, but just by virtue of being myself, I pissed them off. I challenged them and voted against their budgets—because they wanted to segregate things. Men and women couldn't go on trips together. Men and women couldn't socialize together. I was against that. In my mind, we were all adults and capable both of behaving ourselves and of making decisions for ourselves.

One day, the student government asked the head of the student body if we could have a room to meet at the school so we could plan upcoming activities and a trip to a summer camp. No problem. Sweet. He gave us a room on the day of a soccer game between two rival Egyptian teams—no one would be on campus, which was normal for the day of a match like that. Everyone always skipped school to watch them play.

They gave us a room at the end of the hall on the fifth floor of the building.

We didn't think anything of it.

Between a dozen and fifteen of us, men and women, gathered in that room. We talked about how to prepare for our trip and how to raise money.

And then between seventy and eighty members of the Muslim Brotherhood stormed into the room and beat the fuck out of us. All of us, men and women.

There was no one on campus because of the game, so no one could hear us. Our room was at the end of a hallway, so there was no way out. We could either jump out of a fifth-story window or get our asses whipped.

It was strategic. That's when I realized I wasn't fighting a bunch of thugs: I was fighting an organization. It was orchestrated—so orchestrated that I began to think of them as the "Devil's Brotherhood." Who but the devil could plan so well?

Two or three other guys and I got it the worst—I'm not sure why.

We went to the hospital at the university—I felt as if I had a broken rib. Normally, the doctor was supposed to examine us and report our injuries. But the doctor was Muslim Brotherhood. He determined that we had minor bruises, which meant we couldn't file a police report.

I went home, and I couldn't tell my dad I had been beaten pretty badly, but he was a smart guy—he could tell something was up—so I eventually had to tell him.

"Stay away from all of these people," he told me. "They're just thugs."

I could tell he feared that this wouldn't be the end of it and that things could get worse.

"If you're in a situation where you have no choice but to fight, you take the first punch," my dad said. "Don't let them hit you first." He advised me to always punch first. "But eighty of them and fifteen of you? You put yourself in this situation. Stay away from all of these things—it's not worth it."

The government was corrupt, the country was messed up, and none of it was worth it, he told me. This was his way of saying, "This is not going to take you anywhere. You cannot fight this."

That night, I couldn't breathe because every time I inhaled, pain sliced through my ribs.

The next day, the Muslim Brotherhood guys hung signs all around campus accusing us of beating them up. They said that when they walked into the room, they found men and women acting inappropriately and that we then attacked them—we attacked the Muslim Brotherhood—because they called us out for acting inappropriately. They turned it around completely—they said there were only ten of them and one hundred of us. Their public relations person, really, twisted everything, and people believed them over us because they were a religious organization.

The dean of the university, who was not Muslim Brotherhood, got involved.

"You're going to file a police report," he told us. "I'm not going to let those thugs run you out that way."

But after we filed our police report, the Muslim Brotherhood guys filed a police report against us.

We ultimately were expected to go to court because we all had cases against each other. I was advised to drop my case, but I didn't want to drop my case. Everybody knew the Muslim Brotherhood guys were lying, but the system—the government—did nothing. They treated it like just a bunch of college kids beating each other up.

We went to the district attorney's office, and they questioned both me and one of the guys who beat me up. I'm five feet, one inch. I weighed about 112 pounds then. The guy who accused me of beating him up? He was six feet, four inches. "If I can beat up this guy, he's got some issues," I said. "He's twice my size."

"But he filed a police report against you," the district attorney said. "And you filed one against him. If you both drop it, you can go on your happy ways."

We both dropped our complaints.

I need to get the fuck out of here, I thought. *This isn't how I want to spend my life.*

I talked to one of the guys who beat us up.

"Dude," I said. "You guys came and beat us. And then you said we attacked you and that we were doing inappropriate things. You said there were only ten of you. You flipped the whole thing—you're lying."

"The Prophet allows lying in three situations," the guy told me. "One of them is war."

I've never forgotten that—what he had learned from the Muslim Brotherhood. They had already declared war on the government and people of Egypt and, ultimately, the world. This was not my Islam, but understanding that it was theirs would serve me well later.

My second year at college, everyone asked me if I was going to run for student government again. "Fuck all of you," I said. "I'm out." I no longer had any interest in doing any of those things. I already planned to leave Egypt.

To where? Didn't care. Somewhere else.

If I had stayed, I would have had to serve in a military that supported a corrupt government. I knew what was right, and that was not.

That year, 1991, my friends decided to travel to Europe and

get jobs for the summer. But Europe decided not to issue visas because of Desert Storm. Instead, we went to the American embassy to fill out their application—but the visa fee was like seven dollars.

I didn't have it. My pockets were empty. I did not have a penny.

The previous summer, the Americans had decided to defend Kuwait in the Persian Gulf War, with Egypt's support. The Muslim Brotherhood demonstrated against the war. They burned the American flag and cursed the US military.

I figured there was no way in hell the United States would issue a visa to me even as the country flew the last of its troops home from Saudi Arabia, so I basically gave up. My brother—the one my dad had forced me to give half of my garlic-selling salary to—forced seven bucks on me.

"Take it, man," he said. "They might give it to you."

There were three of us—three friends who wanted to go to the United States—and we figured the one rich guy in our group would be the one to get a visa.

We were wrong.

None of us could have known that five years later, I would defend the same flag my classmates had burned.

ME AND THE OTHER guy who wasn't rich, Mohamed, had gotten the visas to come to the US.

Just like my father before me, I needed to leave the place of my birth to look for a better life.

All through my youth, because he loved me, my father had filled me with strong words about family, community, politics, religion, and love. His words about "home" will never leave me: "Your country is the country that gives you your rights and dignity," my father said. "You make that your home."

It was in my DNA to leave, to look for better opportunities. I knew that if I stayed in Egypt, I would always be fighting.

Just as my brother had given me the money for my visa application, my sister lent me $500 to go to the States because I had nothing. I put the $500 in my shoe because I was so afraid someone would steal it. My mom—it was so hard for her to send off her youngest child, but she knew it was the best thing for me. She paid for my airfare.

Just a week after we got the visas, we arrived in New York City. It was July 1991, and I was just twenty years old.

We didn't know what we were doing—we were just kids with no overseas travel experience. I had never been on an airplane. But we knew we couldn't stay in Egypt, and we knew we had been handed a chance.

On the plane, I sat next to an old guy who was extremely nice to me, just friendly and helpful. He spoke fluent Arabic.

He told me his Jewish Egyptian family had been forced out of Egypt in the 1960s. After the Egyptian Revolution of 1952—a coup d'état that saw King Farouk overthrown and that the CIA allegedly knew by the codename "Operation Fat Fucker"[9]—Egypt went through a period of heavy nationalism. It was a reaction, in part, to Israel's creation in 1948, when bombs were also set off in Cairo's Jewish quarter, killing more than seventy people. As wars developed, and continued, between Egypt and Israel, and as Western nations showed support for Israel, Egypt's President Gamal Abdel Nasser declared in 1956 that all Jews were enemies of the state and began to force them to leave. About 450 Jewish businesses were confiscated.[10]

---

9 Bruce Riedel, *Beirut 1958: How America's Wars in the Middle East Began* (Washington, DC: Brookings Institution Press, 2020), 14, online sample, https://www.brookings.edu/wp-content/uploads/2019/04/9780815737292_ch1.pdf.
10 Pablo Jairo Tutillo Maldonado, "How Should We Remember the Forced Migration of Jews from Egypt?," Henry M. Jackson School of International Studies, Stroum Center for Jewish Studies, University of Washington, March 27, 2019, https://jewishstudies

By 2020, only ten Jewish people remained in Alexandria.[11] There had once been eighty thousand Jewish people in the country. When I was growing up, it had been easy to think of Jews as "other"—I didn't know any Jewish people.

But this guy on the plane held no bitterness. He told me he was taking refurbished medical equipment back to Egypt and selling it cheaply as a way to try to help the country—which he and his family still considered their home.

When we arrived in Rome to transfer flights, he held my hand to show me which terminal I needed to fly out of to get to the States. Keep in mind that I looked like a little kid. He was going to Washington, DC. I was going to New York City.

After showing me where I needed to go, he gave me his phone number.

"Hey, when you get to the States, if you need anything, call me," he said.

I remember working it through my mind: He was kind. It must have been a trick. He might be trying to hurt me.

This guy's Jewish, I thought. *He must be the enemy.*

As he walked away in the airport, I tossed his card in the trash. I was a brainwashed fool.

As it turned out, I shouldn't have been turning down help from anyone.

I had never seen rain in July. In Egypt, it just doesn't happen.

.washington.edu/global-judaism/how-we-remember-forced-migration-jews-egypt-1956/.

11 Declan Walsh and Ronen Bergman, "A Bittersweet Homecoming for Egypt's Jews," *New York Times*, February 23, 2020, https://www.nytimes.com/2020/02/23/world/middleeast/a-bittersweet-homecoming-for-egypts-jews.html.

Alexandria's the wettest place in Egypt, but it still only gets seven inches of rain a year—compared to between twenty-eight and sixty-two in New York.

But when we arrived in New York, the rain poured down.

That was the first of many disorienting things. I don't know what we expected—that the United States would be the same as Egypt except in English with a lot of white people? That those people would all look as if they had arrived from the sets of *Dynasty* and *The Dukes of Hazzard*?

We took a bus from the terminal to the subway. I tried to explain to the bus driver that we wanted to go to the YMCA—I had a booklet with all of the YMCAs in the United States. I didn't speak any English. He, as it turned out, didn't speak any Arabic. Finally, the bus driver took the booklet from me and showed us where to go.

We got on the subway, and Mohamed, my friend, lit up a cigarette. Everyone stared at us.

Fresh off the boat. FOB.

"Why is everyone staring at us?"

"Do you think it's because of the cigarette?"

In Egypt, everyone smoked—everywhere. We finally got off the subway, but we didn't know how to get out of the subway station.

The turnstiles at the exits? No clue. Adding to the confusion, it was Sunday, so some were locked. We wandered back and forth and around for a good forty-five minutes before a nice police officer tried to explain it to us.

And then tried again.

When he finally realized that I was a FOB, he took me by the hand—again, because I looked like a little kid—to the exit and helped me through.

When we finally made it to the Y, with the help of many more nice, irritated New Yorkers, we realized just how different things were in the United States. In the Middle East, the Y was a nice place to stay.

In 1991 in New York City, the Y was not the nicest place to stay. The West Side YMCA was—and still is—just off Central Park in the Lincoln Square neighborhood in the middle of low-income housing. I hadn't seen anything like it before—certainly not in Hollywood movies. A year before, I had watched *Pretty Woman*, with Richard Gere and Julia Roberts. I expected clean streets, pretty women, and stretch limos. That's not what I saw, and the poverty, substance abuse, and graffiti scared the fuck out of me.

This was America? This was why I had left Alexandria?

It was one of the most terrifying nights of my life.

Of course, my friend didn't speak any English either, so we had a hard time asking for help. I knew we needed to figure things out quickly because we couldn't afford not to. I did the math in my head: *I've got $500. I've just paid $50 for my first night at the Y. That's ten days, and only if we don't eat.*

Another friend of ours had moved to the States from Egypt a few years before. We found a pay phone inside the Y, and I had our friend's number, but we're talking about a guy who couldn't make his way out of a turnstile. And when our friend's mom gave me his phone number, she didn't write a 1 in front of it.

So I put in the quarter, and I dialed the number. I got the operator. She did not speak my language. So I put in another quarter, and I dialed the number.

And I got the operator.

This went on until three o'clock in the morning.

The pay phones were right near the bathroom, and this guy stood there watching me dialing and dialing and dialing. He looked as if he was on something and maybe had been on something for a while. He looked like he was going to cut me.

"Here," he said. "Let me help you out."

He dialed the number for me.

First day in America, and I'd been helped by the three people I would least expect it from: a Jew, a cop, and a junkie.

I got through to my friend, and it was an ungodly hour. He sounded surprised to hear from me. I told him where I was.

"Stay where you're at," he said. "Don't move. Don't go to the street. Don't talk to anybody. It's dangerous. I'll come get you tomorrow."

So now we were even more terrified. Wet and confused and exhausted and scared after more than twenty hours of travel and no sleep.

When I finally went back to our room, we moved the dresser against the door to make sure that no one could open it from the outside and steal our $450 fortune. To keep it safe, I hid it again in my shoe. We had bunk beds. I think many immigrants coming to America have spent their first night in their new country in a bunk bed at the Y. And it seems funny now, but at the time?

Not funny.

Our friend came the next day and picked us up and took us to New Jersey. There are a lot of FOBs in New Jersey, and they're pretty good about helping one another out—probably because they've all slept in the bunk beds at the Y.

"I know some people—four people—who have an extra room,"

my friend said. "They just had a guy move out. It's only space for one person, but they're willing to have both of you move in."

The rent was like $100 a month for both of us.

He took us to see the room: No bed. No mattress. No linen. Just a room.

We slept on the floor for about three months.

Then the guy who had moved out of the room came back, so we had to move out. This is how we lived for a time: we found pockets of immigrants, four or five of them, and we'd all go in on a house or an apartment together.

We were so poor. In one place, we didn't have a refrigerator, so we sat our perishables on the window ledge. Neither of us were eligible to work yet. One day, we found a mattress that somebody had thrown away, and we brought it home and considered ourselves lucky. We bought a blanket.

Sweet.

Score.

We'd found the American Dream.

But here's the funny thing: even then, even sleeping on the floor without a mattress, even being happy to find somebody else's used mattress, I was grateful for the opportunity to dream.

People take the American Dream for granted: buying a house or buying this or that. For me, the American Dream is simply the right to dream: *Someday, I want to have that house. Someday, I want to have discussions with professors. Someday, I want to be treated with respect.* In America, this was obvious, even in our no-English-speaking, ineligible-for-work, desperately poor state.

In a lot of places in the Middle East, the system is not set up for dreaming—for being afforded an education, for being promoted on the basis of merit, for having a career if you are a woman.

I chose to come here so I could dream. I wanted the opportunity to succeed by using my intelligence and skill, to experience a democracy with its ideas about equality, and to think loudly and freely without fearing the false prophet down the street.

If I had to dream on someone else's used mattress, so be it.

I tell my kids I moved more than fifteen times during those years. I lived in the tiniest places. One landlord wanted to save money, so he turned off the heat at night. Another woman rented me a room that was essentially a closet. It was so tiny that I hung my clothes on the shower curtain rod—there was nowhere else to put them. When I took a shower, I put my clothes on the bed.

Everything was difficult. Getting a driver's license. Figuring out breakfast. What in the actual hell is a blueberry pancake? I grew up eating falafel and hard cheeses and flatbread for breakfast. The bakery sweets and cereals turned my stomach.

But there was a huge Egyptian population in Jersey City, as well as a mosque. It's like anywhere: if you moved to Yemen tomorrow, you would pretty quickly figure out where the Americans hang out, and that's where you would go. That's what I did.

In Jersey City, new immigrants could—and still can—get a job, go to school, and go to the mosque.

But I'll be damned if that mosque wasn't just a direct extension of what I had encountered at home. The mosque wasn't a grand, large building with a rounded roof—it was a hole in the wall. It sat about half a mile from the train station in Jersey City in a row of connected buildings. We took the narrow stairs to the second floor, which had a couple of big rooms, and that was the mosque. People walking past would never notice it.

It was right across the street from the Army recruiting center—which was a bit more obvious.

At the mosque I found . . . the Blind Sheikh. That's Omar Abdel-Rahman, the same dude I had heard about as a kid in Alexandria, the one who recorded sermons on cassette tapes and ordered the fatwa against Egypt's president.

After his jail time back home for being involved in the death of Sadat, Egypt booted him out. He spent some time in Afghanistan, and then in 1990, he struck out for Jersey City on a tourist visa issued to him by the US embassy in Sudan—even though he was on the terrorist watch list. Somebody realized there had been a screwup, and they revoked his visa.

And issued him a green card.

In Jersey.[12]

The CIA had then approved his visa.

How stupid could you be that you'd let that guy preach here? I thought. I couldn't believe it. *Is anyone paying attention?*

I quickly figured out that most of America didn't want to know us—didn't want to know the dishwashers and taxi drivers and house cleaners. They only wanted to see us when they needed us. They didn't care about our families or our religions or our homes.

That shit will keep biting us in the ass until we recognize that immigrants are part of us, that they need to be included—and

---

12 Bill Trott, "'Blind Sheikh' Convicted in 1993 World Trade Bombing Dies in U.S. Prison," Reuters, February 18, 2017, https://www.reuters.com/article/us-usa-tradecenter -rahman/blind-sheikh-convicted-in-1993-world-trade-bombing-dies-in-u-s-prison -idUSKBN15X0KU.

that including them makes our lives richer and safer. Not including them—not learning about their dreams or their needs or their stories—allows the terrorists to move freely among us and also keeps them hidden.

Just before I arrived in New York, in 1990, an Egyptian who followed the Blind Sheikh became part of the first extremist Muslim cell—five brainwashed Egyptian guys—in the United States. When El Sayyid Nosair arrived here, he worked at an electrical plant. But after being electrocuted on the job,[13] he became disabled, impotent, depressed, and jobless. He had campaigned to bring the Blind Sheikh to the United States in the first place.

Nosair was accused of killing Meir Kahane, who was a far-right Israeli politician and cofounder of the Jewish Defense League. Kahane was no great shakes either, as far as practicing loving kindness, and liked to lecture about expelling all Palestinians from Israel.

The Blind Sheikh visited Nosair in jail, and Osama bin Laden donated $20,000 to his defense fund. Nosair was acquitted of Kahane's murder—his lawyer argued it wasn't his gun.

However, Nosair later admitted to disguising himself as a Sephardic Jew, attending a lecture, and twice shooting Kahane in the jugular before yelling, "It's Allah's will!"[14] Being not bright, he got into the wrong getaway cab, told the driver to stop, and got into another car after first shooting a US Postal Service police officer. His pals left him bleeding in the street after he was also

---

13 Mark S. Hamm, *Crimes Committed by Terrorist Groups: Theory, Research and Prevention*, Final Report (Terre Haute, IN: Criminology Department, Indiana State University, 2005), 33, https://www.ojp.gov/pdffiles1/nij/grants/211203.pdf.

14 Hamm, *Crimes Committed by Terrorist Groups*, 36.

shot. Martyr and so on. But he lived, and police found military documents, as well as a map of the World Trade Center, when they searched his apartment.

In the early 1990s, the Blind Sheikh raised money in New York and sent it back to Egypt, along with messages to his followers about whom they should target next. In Brooklyn, he recorded more cassette tapes with the usual antisemitic tripe, which he used to justify another fatwa in 1990: It's okay to kill Jews in the United States. Go ahead and rob some banks, too. He told Muslims—the extremist ones who listened to his bullshit—to attack the West, destroy the economy, and shoot at planes. He said that the infidels should be murdered and that Egypt should become an Islamic state—whatever that means. It was already Islamic in my mind, and it did not have to be like Saudi Arabia or Iran to be Islamic. Islam is a way of life and certainly does not need to be extreme. But the Blind Sheikh sent his cassette tapes back to Egypt, where tens of thousands of followers listened to them. The tapes traveled from Egypt all across Africa, where I would encounter them yet again.

Obviously, I didn't know any of that at the time. I just knew the Blind Sheikh was a bad man.

This is really interesting, I thought when I stumbled upon him at the mosque. *Let's see what this clown has to say.*

Of course, I kept in mind the lessons of my father—and the nonsense tapes I had heard as a kid.

The Blind Sheikh would sit at the mosque, and people would ask him questions. He would answer from his own religious perspective. This dude was supposed to be like the wise guru who sits at the top of the mountain meditating and waiting for people to show up and ask questions after an excruciating journey to get there. They called him a scholar.

First question: Is oral sex forbidden?

Seriously? This is what you guys come to ask the man you see as the wisest of the wise?

The scholar talked about marital relationships and oral sex for about fifteen minutes.

Here we are, at the mosque, and these guys are wondering about blow jobs. They could ask him the meaning of life. They could ask him how the Prophet would have lived in modern times. They could ask him how to best live as a good Muslim. They could ask how to be a good Muslim and a good American and a good Egyptian—while still serving God.

Nope.

Oral sex.

I'm sitting in the wrong place, I thought.

For that, I thank my father. In life, we are presented with options, and we must decide what we accept and what we reject. That's the same for all cultures: Do we want to be in a church that is racist? Do we want to be in a church that is exclusionary? Do we want to be in a church that is extremist? Everyone who goes to church has a reason they choose that particular church.

I chose against this man and his false narrative.

And not because he said oral sex was haram. In fact, he said oral sex was perfectly okay.

So now you know.

Some people did pay attention—and did offer warnings about the Blind Sheikh's militancy—including an Egyptian official who said in 1993 that the sheikh used New York as a base to raise money and send messages to Egypt telling his followers whom to target. The official said he didn't understand why the United States had let him into the country.[15]

But even as I was rejecting militant Islam, I encountered my own issues with stereotypes.

When I arrived in the United States, I planned to get a student visa. I went to Hunter College in New York City to learn English.

But I needed a job.

First, I worked in a factory that made handbags. The owner was Syrian.

"You're a Muslim," he said. "We're brothers. We'll take care of you."

Every day, I worked from 9:00 a.m. to 5:00 p.m. making handbags. Every evening, I went to school.

The smell of leather from the factory never left my skin. At school, the smell emanated from my pores. But there was a JCPenney at the top of one of the subway stations between work and school—I think at Seventh Avenue and Thirty-First Street in New York. I stopped every day and sprayed myself with a sample bottle of cologne.

Everybody always told me I smelled good.

After six months, the factory owed me about $8,000.

My Muslim brothers didn't pay me. I was desperate—I had just enough from a second job to keep me mostly fed, but I needed to figure out how to pay for school.

Sometimes it feels as if the entire world is going against you,

15 Chris Hedges, "A Cry of Islamic Fury, Taped in Brooklyn for Cairo," *New York Times*, January 7, 1993, https://www.nytimes.com/1993/01/07/world/a-cry-of-islamic-fury-taped-in-brooklyn-for-cairo.html.

but you just need to suck it up and keep moving. Soon after I arrived in the US, I went for a walk and some asshole robbed me. I didn't even have anything for him to take, but the dude hit me in the head with a beer bottle, and I had to go to the hospital to take care of a concussion and get a couple of stitches.

"You should go back to Egypt," my brother said.

My friend who had traveled with me from Egypt went home a week after I was robbed.

As luck would have it, at about the same time, I got a terrible toothache. I found a guy who did dentistry in his house.

"We're going to have to take it out," he told me.

This guy had pliers. No pain meds, no anesthesia. Afterward, I bled for three days, so I went back.

"Oh!" the guy said. "We need to stitch it."

Preparation. Each of us—everyone in the Unit—has a story of pain or trauma or challenge.

I worked at least ten different jobs in those first couple of years in the States. I worked nights at a gas station. I worked in a bakery, where I had to clean a freezer. After spending ten minutes inside it, I thought I would die of hypothermia. I started delivering cakes and bread to hotels, working a shift from 2:00 a.m. to 7:00 a.m. every day.

When I look back, some things barely feel real. You know those guys in Times Square who play chess at the concrete tables? Those guys play for money. When I was really, really hurting for money to buy food, I would play chess. Even though I couldn't speak English, the guys at the tables never turned me away. I would make just enough, a couple of bucks, to get some dinner and take the train home.

Some nights, for dinner, I made tomato sandwiches because I didn't have any money.

For someone new to this country, each of these things was hard. When you want that dream bad enough, you do the hard things. Sometimes, it feels almost as if you're being punished for dreaming so hard.

You will find a way.

At the gas station, my boss skimmed money off the top—he told me it was for taxes. And it was October and getting cold outside. I needed a warmer gig. On Broadway Street, in Bayonne, New Jersey, there are blocks and blocks of stores, so one day, I started on Fifty-Fifth Street and walked up Broadway, knocking on every door looking for a job. Thirty blocks in, Jim opened the door of his clothing store. He hired me for one day. I did a good job. He gave me a job for a week. And then he hired me. He was professional, kind. He gave me raises without me asking, as well as Christmas bonuses and time off for Ramadan. And we'd go for lunch together. He had an accent, so I finally asked him where he was from.

"*Habibi!*" he said. "I'm your cousin!"

"What do you mean?" I asked.

"I'm Jewish!" he said.

And then, "Do you have an issue with it?"

I didn't even have to think about it.

"You're nice to me," I said. "You pay me on time. No, I don't have an issue. You're Jewish, but where are you from?"

"I'm from Israel," he said.

"You're not just a cousin," I said. "You're a cousin and an enemy."

And he laughed, and I laughed, and we ate the lunch that he paid for. He had served in the Israeli Army—in Egypt. On paper, you don't get any more different from that. But in reality, we were the same. It was as if a light switch went off. I worked for him for three years. He trusted me and I trusted him 100 percent.

He was my friend.

We both had immigrated to the States, and we ended up helping each other out. One day, the bank repossessed his car. He called me to ask for a ride. And when I joined the Army, I sought his advice.

His mother once came to the store. She was an older lady, and she looked like an Arab. She told me about the food she ate, and it was like talking to my mother. They could have been sisters. They dressed the same; they acted the same; they talked the same.

Life becomes more interesting when you stop seeing people as different.

My older brother, an engineer, also came to the States. He knew how to speak English, and he looked European, with blond hair and green eyes.

I, on the other hand, looked like an immigrant. When I arrived in the United States, I didn't know how to drive. I didn't know how to speak English. I didn't know anything.

I had asked my brother to teach me to drive, and he yelled at me as I was driving, which has never, in the decades and generations of new drivers, been an effective way to teach someone how to drive. I said, "Screw it," or something along those lines, and our lessons stopped.

As I worked one day in the ladies' department for Jim, he asked if I could drive.

Me? Of course I can drive.

He asked me to drive to our other store. To get there, I had to take Route 22 in New Jersey, which is a truck route. If I went, he'd give me an extra dollar an hour for transportation. That was a lot for me.

The whole time I drove—probably thirty-five miles per hour—I ducked in my seat as the semis whizzed by me.

Man, this is where I'm going to die, I thought.

I didn't die.

And I got my five bucks.

On February 26, 1993, as I hung dresses from a rack, Jim and I heard news that pulled us together to listen to the radio. Someone had driven a truck filled with explosives into the parking garage of the World Trade Center.

Please, God, don't let it be Muslim terrorists, I thought. That was always my first thought, is always my first thought, as a Muslim man living in America.

My second thought? I worried about the building and the people in it: I adored the World Trade Center. It represented everything American to me. We both felt great relief when we realized the terrorist hadn't pulled off what he'd meant to do.

As we listened, I understood that Jim and I felt the same things: Concern for our fellow citizens. Anger at whoever had tried to hurt our country. The gut-sinking fear as we waited for numbers of deaths and estimates of damage.

Jim had a lot of Muslim friends, and he worried about them.

"This is not what Islam should look like," he said. He knew the impact the attack would have on us—and understood that Judaism and Christianity shouldn't be about stigmatizing a group of people for the actions of a few. For some reason, it never seemed to apply in the opposite direction: no one saw all white, Christian Army vets as evil after Timothy McVeigh appeared in Oklahoma City.

That was the first time I started passing as Hispanic. If people didn't ask—if people assumed—I let them think what they wanted to think. But I also started to change the way I thought.

After spending time with Jim, and with friends from school and friends from work, I started to see the world from a different optic.

It opened my mind. I started thinking, *Okay, this guy is being nice, and he does not look like what the media in Egypt portrays.* The guy from Argentina who was Jewish and was going to school with me had the same struggles I had: How do you save money for school? How do you get a job in the evening to pay for this?

I realized we were all the same. We all had the same goals. We were all looking for security.

We wanted a better life.

There were other things I loved about America.

I barely understood what I saw on the news, but I understood that people daily questioned the politicians, officials, and even the police who ran the country. People with differing viewpoints debated everything from religion to who made the best pizza— without fear of a beating from thugs.

I started to want more. My English improved. I taught myself to drive. And I felt as if I had a debt to pay to my chosen country.

So in 1994, I went back to that mosque in Jersey where I had seen the Blind Sheikh.

And I walked across the street to the recruiter's office.

DURING MY FIRST DAY in the Army, at Fort Jackson, South Carolina, when we all had to introduce ourselves, I said I was Egyptian American.

"I thought we killed all you guys during Desert Storm." That's what my drill sergeant said to me.

Later, I thought maybe this was an ignorant way to try to break me in.

His shit? Not my problem. I had a dream.

I showed up at the recruiting station with a friend.

I wanted to join the Navy, but the Navy guy wasn't there. The Army guy was there.

The recruiter looked at me and my friend.

"Are you gay?" he asked.

"What?" I said, confused by every aspect of the question. "No! He's just my friend."

Bill Clinton had just approved the "don't ask, don't tell" act, but this was not information I had gained during the little time I had between three jobs and college.

By the time I did understand why the recruiter would ask that, I also better understood discrimination and how detrimental it could be in the workplace—and to national security.

The recruiter had me take the ASVAB—the military's test to determine where your strengths are and whether you're smart enough to be able to follow an order—and, surprisingly, I passed.

"You can join," the recruiter told me. "Your English sucks, but your math is great." I didn't miss any math questions, and usually, they would put me in maybe engineering or accounting. I wanted to be a communications guy.

They said I had to be in administration because I wasn't a citizen. The Army decided it would be best for me to learn how to type.

Jim, of course, was one of the first people I told, and he immediately made sure I understood the ins and outs of being recruited: Make sure you get your college money. Tell them you want to finish your semester at college. Don't let them sign you up as a cook.

But my other friends and my family tried to discourage me, saying, "This is against your religion."

When that argument didn't work, they said, "They're going to break your arm because you're brown."

One friend—a big guy going to college for accounting—asked me why I wanted to join the Army.

"This is like paying your debt in advance," I told him. "You have to earn your right to be an American, and I am going to earn it now by serving."

He thought this was crazy and more than a little stupid.

It's the strangest question to me: "Why did you join the military?"

Why didn't you?

I figured we'd only go after bad guys, so no good guys would be killed. Joining would provide me a true opportunity to move forward—to succeed in my new country. But most importantly, joining the military would allow me to have the most impact I could have as an American.

My dad definitely didn't want me to join—he was still in protection mode. I was the youngest, and I looked even younger than I was.

"Someone is going to kill you," my dad said.

I worried more about whether I would be big enough to join. To join the Army, I had to be at least five feet tall and weigh ninety-three pounds. Golden. I was in by an inch and a few pounds.

They make you do some weird things to make sure your body operates correctly. You go through with a group of people, and they check your heart and do some blood tests and listen to your lungs. At one point, they put all the guys in a room, dressed only in our underwear, and made us walk like a duck.

I've never been so scared of walking like a duck in my life.

I thought for sure they were going to notice where the tractor ran over my foot because, to this day, there's still a scar.

"Have you ever had any injuries?"

"Nope."

"Asthma?"

"Nope."

"Ever fall into a canal and almost drown?"

"Nope, nope, and nope."

In my mind, the tractor injury didn't hold me back. Just like the farm and the vegetable cart and the escapade at the beach, it toughened me for the path ahead.

On my green card, they misspelled my name. I think the lady did it intentionally—I have an unusual last name, and the new name looked as if it could be Spanish or Italian. "It's easier to change your Social Security card than your green card, so let's just change your Social Security card," my recruiter said. He wanted to meet his quota.

This is how I, like thousands of immigrants before me, got a new name.

It was the first of many new names for me.

Muhammad. The Mexican. Camel jockey.

Adam.

At basic training, I encountered more toughening. When I told the other guys what my job would be, I always got the same response: "Admin is for girls."

Did they expect me to say infantry? I looked fourteen.

It didn't matter. I knew I was where I was supposed to be. And honestly, eating sand (doing push-ups) in a pit on my first day of work wasn't worse than spending my first night in New York City at the Y with a dresser pushed against the door.

But in New York, I had been able to find people who looked like me—even people who spoke my language. There was a shared experience. At basic training, nobody looked like me. Nobody sounded like me.

But I lucked out with my bunkmate. My battle buddy—a tall white guy from Pennsylvania named Gilmore—tried to apologize for what the drill sergeant said about killing all the Arabs. He got it. From that day on, he tried to help me daily, acting as my translator.

One of my drill sergeants was a guy from Alabama. He barked orders at us, and I didn't understand anything—his accent or his words.

"What's a latrine?"

"What's a chow hall?"

"What's a canteen?"

Gilmore explained.

In Egypt, we say, "Do a good deed and throw it in the sea"—do something for the joy of doing it, not because you expect something in return—but I like to think about Gilmore having an excellent life somewhere because of what he did for me.

"Man, what did the drill sergeant just say?" I'd ask—all too often.

"I didn't understand him," Gilmore would say. And then I'd feel good, because if he couldn't understand him either, I was fine. We just followed everybody else. This guy's moving this way, so we'll move this way.

Gilmore couldn't always save me.

I didn't know what earplugs were.

The drill sergeant said, "Say 'earplugs.'"

"Say earplugs," I said.

"No," he said. "Say 'earplugs,' private."

"Say earplugs."

It was like an Abbott and Costello skit from the 1930s: "Who's on first?"

They evaluated me to see if I needed English as a Second Language remedial training, but I had memorized the Smart Book— the book of all the skills you have to learn in basic training. I could recite back anything, even if I didn't have a clue what it meant.

Gilmore and I got pretty close. I was behind in language, but I was still able to help him out sometimes, too. I mean, I really knew that Smart Book.

"I will not quit my post until properly relieved."

"When face paint sticks are not issued, burnt cork or charcoal can be used to tone down exposed skin."

"Effective range: 800 meters."

Gilmore and I also told each other stories and supported each other and laughed at the stupid things and reminded each other that it was all just a head game: The fire drills in the middle of the night. The constant yelling. Waiting for an hour only to be told we now had only thirty seconds to accomplish a task.

Breaking us down to build us up.

One week, they asked if any of us would like to go to Sunday service. Even people who weren't religious tended to go because it was a change of scenery and no one would make us mop floors or do push-ups at services.

They dropped me off for Catholic service. I sat through an hour of Mass having no idea what was happening.

"What's wrong with you?" a drill sergeant asked.

"Well," I said, "I'm not Christian."

"What the fuck are you then?" he asked.

"I'm Muslim," I said.

"Well, why did they drop you off here?"

"I don't know."

The next week, he dropped me off at the Islamic services.

But I learned that 90 percent of what they said at the Catholic services was the same as what they said at the mosque. And I didn't stick out. I looked like I belonged. When I went to the mosque, it had blonds and Blacks, and it wasn't all guys who looked like me.

Once again, my world expanded. I saw how it could look.

I also faced reminders of just how small my world was, even with family and friends spread around the world. Every week, we could stand in line—like sixty of us—parade rest, legs wide, arms akimbo, on a concrete slab waiting for one of two or three pay phones pinned to a brick wall. At that time, making a call to Egypt from a pay phone cost a fortune.

Also, my family didn't have a phone.

At mail call every evening, the whole company would gather round for the drill sergeant to call out names. We'd all crowd in there, stinky after a day of training, hoping for a letter or a package. And everybody got something at least occasionally.

Except for me.

Mailing a letter from Egypt was also expensive—and unlikely to ever make it out of the post office. If it did arrive, it might be long after I had left Fort Jackson.

So every day, I just sat there watching everybody else get mail. *Can we just maybe make this whole distribution thing go by real quick?*

Same with the phone calls. I mean, I didn't want anyone to feel bad for me, but basic training is about as lonely as you can get (while sleeping in a room with fifty-nine other dudes). We all second-guessed our decisions. The guy on the next bunk over is an asshole. (There's always an asshole.) My drill sergeant's talking about killing Muslims. We're singing cadences about wanting to go home. Home has the best pastries and the best beach and the best mom and it's 6,068 miles away.

"Smith?"

"Jones?"

"Alphabet?"

"Alphabet?"

"Kowalcyzk?"

But never "Gamal."

Everybody's family came to graduation. Obviously, if I wasn't getting letters and I didn't have anyone to call, probably no one was going to show up for graduation.

My battle buddy? The tall red-headed farm kid from Pennsylvania? He kept looking out for me.

"My family is your family," he said. "You can spend the day with us."

I'm still bummed we didn't stay in touch—he was in the reserves, and we just lost contact.

I didn't end up spending the day with his family, though. I thought that would have been a little weird for them. But it was nice of him to ask, and it has stuck with me through the years.

Instead, I went to the mall. It was the first time I had any spending money that didn't have to go toward rent or school. I recently looked at that first Leave and Earnings Statement (LES): $570. Back then, I thought I was rich.

I went straight to a department store, and rather than spray myself with a sampler, I bought my first bottle of cologne.

I had no idea what I would encounter in the Army, but I was going to smell good for it.

THE RECEPTION BUS DROPPED me off at my new unit at 5:00 p.m.

On a Friday.

There was nobody around, and I didn't know what to do. I didn't know where I was going to sleep. I didn't know where I was going to put this big duffel bag full of crap.

My first assignment was in Texas.

I was scared. I looked different. I still got lost easily. I did not yet know how to fake a Hispanic accent, so I was just this brown kid of indeterminate origin floating around in an unknown-to-me neighborhood that maybe wasn't the most welcoming to Muslims.

Fortunately, the S3 (operations officer) just happened to be there. He was a nice major I got to know later.

"What would you do if I wasn't here?" he asked.

Set up my sleeping bag in the hallway for the weekend?

He called a first sergeant, who came and picked me up. He had a two-seater Nissan 360Z, which was a really, really cool car. He stuffed my duffel bag in the back and drove me home purely because I wore the same uniform he did.

I had loved basic training—I kept thinking, *This is really cool training,* even if I didn't understand exactly what was going on. I had never even dreamed about this stuff as a kid in Egypt, and I didn't take any of it for granted. But when I started interacting with people, like the first sergeant who didn't know me but took me to his house, that's when I started to understand that the military was a family. That first sergeant didn't know who I was. I was a private. I needed to eat, and I needed a place to sleep. He didn't know my religion, my name, my ethnic background—nothing.

All of a sudden, I was part of a tribe. He was an African American guy—First Sergeant Jones—and I remember him vividly. That was more than twenty-five years ago.

I mention that he was African American because for me, as a brown guy, I could see his success. I'm sure I didn't think of it in specific terms at the time, but looking back, I learned early that any of us, no matter where we came from, could go far. We were part of something bigger. I was so glad I decided that, even though I could barely speak English, I would rather be a soldier than a taxi driver. And I was so grateful that I had that choice.

I wanted to be in Jones's company, but when he took me in Monday morning, I had already been assigned to a different company. He handed me over to Sergeant First Class Green.

"Are you scared?" Green asked.

Yes. Yes, I am.

"You shouldn't be scared about anything," he said.

From there, he taught me that all that mattered was how well I did my job. Even better, he taught me that's all that matters about anybody.

I learned a lot about military family in that unit and from Sergeant First Class Green.

I worked with a woman who dated women, and this was during the time of the "don't ask, don't tell" policy, which meant the military wasn't supposed to ask people if they were gay and service members weren't supposed to tell their bosses if they were gay. But if anyone found out a person was gay, then they could be booted out of the military. It was a purely political decision—most people in the military seemed not to care, but politicians outside the military decided we couldn't serve together without bad behavior. President Clinton made this deal with the devil to calm people, but it meant that people who served—who agreed to fight this nation's battles, possibly giving up their lives for that agreement—couldn't live authentically. This woman couldn't bring her partner to a barbecue or receive flowers at work or talk about her weekend. It was dehumanizing, and it could be used in vengeful ways. Don't like your boss? Turn him in. Do something wrong? Threaten to out the person who caught you.

In this case, everybody knew she was gay, and nobody cared. She did her job well, and we liked her. We couldn't ask her about her family because we didn't want to get her in trouble, and we thought of her as part of our military family, which, now that I think about it, is about the most ridiculous sentence I've ever written.

And yeah, I learned from the bad, too.

My team sergeant was a super nice guy from maybe West Virginia or Kentucky or someplace like that. He had this soft, semi-southern accent, and he walked with a hitch, sort of pushing his right shoulder forward—like he was tough, which made me laugh. Super fit. He was one of only a few guys in our unit who had served in Desert Storm in 1991, where, like everybody else, he learned to dehumanize "the enemy." In Germany, they called everybody "Heinrich." Japan? Well. They put Japanese Americans in camps and took away their homes and called them "Japs" and worse. Somalia? "Skinnies."

They did it in Desert Storm, too: "Achmed" and "Muhammad" and whatever. "Should bomb the whole country into glass."

When this sergeant got home from Desert Storm, just like service members in previous generations, he didn't let it go—not that I was thinking any of this or even knew any of it, at that point. He was just my team sergeant.

For two or three weeks, he referred to me as "camel jockey."

Between the accent, the context, and the unknown term, I had no idea what he was saying. "Yes, sergeant," I'd reply to whatever had come before "camel jockey," and I'd move on.

Finally, my squad leader heard him call me "camel jockey," pulled him aside, and chewed him inside out.

"Hey," my squad leader said to me, "if anybody says something like that to you again and it offends you, let me know."

But I didn't understand what the fuck he was saying.

Everybody kept talking about how offended I was.

"What's a 'camel jockey'?" I asked.

They explained it to me. Oddly enough, no one uses that term in Egypt.

"He shouldn't be calling you that."

"Oh."

They made him apologize to me, and I told him I wasn't offended, because I didn't know what the fuck he was talking about, especially with his accent.

"But," I said, "don't call me that again. Apparently, it's offensive."

We were fine after that. I honestly don't think he meant anything by it, and it simply hadn't occurred to him that I would be offended. I did see, sometimes in the military, that people would say racist things, but they seemed to think that, as long as they said those racist things to you directly, it was okay. Obviously, he wasn't being racist if he called me "camel jockey" to my face, right?

He was learning, and I was learning, and I was also trying to learn everything about everything in an environment that was new in every single way. I have no doubt that people have allowed me moments of grace when I have said or done stupid things—they corrected me in a way that allowed me to grow.

That's what I learned early in a good unit with a good command climate—a pocket of good humans—at Fort Hood. It informed the rest of my career.

Green, my platoon sergeant, was a big part of that. He was an Irish American guy, and he took me under his wing. He gave me the foundation I needed to succeed in the Army: he taught me everything, and then he sent me to computer class so I could have an extra skill under my belt. He seemed to understand that I was going to need any extra I could get—but also that I wanted it. I wanted to know everything.

I ran fast, and so did Green, so he took me running with him. You can learn a lot on a long run—from how to process a document to which soldiers you should avoid and why your sergeant joined the Army.

"You're going to go really far in the Army," he told me. "Shine your boots. Get a good haircut. Run fast. Then you're a good soldier."

Those are the essentials.

NINE

FOUR MONTHS AFTER SERGEANT Green picked me up from the orderly room, I found myself in a sea of gray in Bosnia.

I sat there in the rain, and the sky was a dreary mess, and everywhere we went, we saw yellow signs warning of land mines, and the buildings were pocked or simply outlines of their former selves after years of war. The kids wore what they had: shorts and sweaters, wool socks and flip-flops. I felt as if I had been dropped into the aftermath of World War II. The children had dealt with years of trauma: They'd run to school to lessen the chances of a sniper's bullet hitting them. Their fathers had been murdered. Their mothers and sisters had been raped, often multiple times. I watched these kids playing with ChemLights, and I saw soldiers dig around in their MRE (meals ready to eat) packs for peanut butter and M&M's and crackers so they could share their food with them.

Bosnia would teach me big lessons about soldiering, about US policy, about the many flavors of Islam, and about military family. All of those things would directly affect my military career.

More than one hundred thousand people had been killed between 1992 and 1995 during the Bosnian War. After the Soviet Union collapsed in 1991 and a string of communist countries started to tumble, things got particularly ugly in Yugoslavia. Bosnia and Herzegovina (which is now one country, usually referred to as Bosnia, with two regions: Bosnia to the north and Herzegovina to the south) voted for independence in early 1992. Now this was a pretty diverse country: 44 percent Muslim Bosniaks, 33 percent Eastern Orthodox (Christian) Serbs, and 17 percent Catholic Croats. But the Serbs rejected the vote, saying they feared being a minority in a Muslim country, and then attacked the Republic of Bosnia and Herzegovina so they could create their own Serbian state. That included ethnic cleansing—which means they killed or forced out Muslims in that area. This resulted in a war between the Christian Serbs, including support from Slobodan Milosevic's Serbian government, and the Army of the Republic of Bosnia and Herzegovina—which was mostly made up of Muslim Bosniaks—that spread across Bosnia.

In Srebrenica, 73 percent of the population was Bosnian Muslim, and 25 percent was Bosnian Serb. In 1992, the Serbs gave the Muslims twenty-four hours to leave. Through sniper fire and daily shelling, as well as starvation, they ultimately forced seventy thousand Bosniaks out of their homes and destroyed almost three hundred villages.

Men and women were rounded up in villages. The men were either killed in front of their families or taken away and never seen again. There were accusations, and evidence, of mass, systemic rape, particularly by the Serbs but also by everybody else. The European Union reported that twenty thousand women were raped, oftentimes repeatedly.

As the war spread, they shelled the hell out of each other, hitting both military and civilian targets. The war drew international condemnation, in part because of several heartbreaking stories reported by the journalists who flooded the region, as well as, frankly, because people in the West could relate to the people depicted in those stories: they looked European and lived in European-style homes in European-style climates.

There was a beautiful old bridge, Stari Most, built by Suleiman the Magnificent in 1557 in Mostar, which is the unofficial capital of Herzegovina. It was considered a bridge between communities because churches and synagogues and mosques sat near it. The Catholic Croats destroyed it—as well as ten mosques in the city—during the war, even though it had no strategic importance.

And in 1993, a story streamed across the world's news stations about Sarajevo's "Romeo and Juliet"—she a Muslim Bosniak and he a Christian Bosnian Serb. They had dated since they were kids, and their families welcomed one another as future relatives. As the city was under siege, the couple decided to flee, traveling down "Sniper Alley," the main road in Sarajevo. Snipers maintained posts all along the road and tried to kill anyone who ventured out of his or her home, even for groceries. But the couple, believing they had friends in every area of the city, decided to chance it: they would go live with his family. Their friends made an arrangement with the snipers, ensuring they could travel safely at a particular time on a particular day.

As they approached the Vrbanja Bridge, a sniper broke the agreement and shot the man, Boško Brkić. He fell to the ground, dying instantly. Another shot, and she, Admira Ismić, was also hit. She crawled to her boyfriend and embraced him. Witnesses said she lived for another fifteen minutes.

Their bodies remained together, embracing, for seven days.

They were each twenty-five and had been together since they were fifteen, back when their city had been a melting pot of religions and cultures going back five hundred years.

Like Alexandria.

In Srebrenica, in July 1995, after the United Nations had proclaimed it a safe area, more than eight thousand Muslim men and boys were killed. The Serbs attacked two other "safe areas" and planned to take over Sarajevo—a landmark city that Americans could visualize because of the 1984 Olympics held there: Germany's Katarina Witt dancing across the ice to gold in a tiara and a hot-pink skirt. Scott Hamilton taking gold for the Americans in men's figure skating—with the world hoping for his trademark backflip. The Soviet Union's hockey team creaming everyone else just four years after the US team's Miracle on Ice.

Just a decade later, one hundred thousand people were killed, according to the US Holocaust Museum.

After North Atlantic Treaty Organization (NATO) air strikes on 338 targets from August through September, representatives from the three factions agreed to meet. Ultimately, the United States led peace negotiations, the Dayton Agreement, in Ohio in the fall of 1995. There, they decided to create two republics, the Bosnian-

Croat Federation of Bosnia and Herzegovina and the Bosnian Serb Republic. Each would have its own government, but they would report to a central government that would rotate its presidency every eight months among a Serb, a Bosniak, and a Croat.

To enforce the accord, NATO sent in sixty thousand peacekeepers, including a kid from Egypt who learned an early lesson on that deployment: the United States—and the rest of its allies, for that matter—was going in to support a Muslim population. This was pre-9/11, and the response might have been different under a nationalist president, as we saw in 2019 when the Kurds were abandoned to the Turks in Syria. But in 1995, twenty thousand Americans, as well as forty thousand of their allies, were going in to help, and it didn't matter that the aggressors were Christian and the victims were Muslim.

Americans had been in Bosnia since December 1995, so we went in as replacements to maintain the peace in 1996.

As we got ready to deploy back home in Texas, Sergeant First Class Green gave me a laptop so I could do my admin job.

I've made it, I thought. *I have a laptop.*

But when we got to Bosnia, I quickly realized I had aspirations that went far beyond a keyboard.

I never wanted to be an admin guy. Who joins the Army to type letters? I joined the Army to do Army stuff, but I couldn't get a security clearance because I wasn't a US citizen.

I hadn't done any military police (MP) training before that deployment. When we got to Bosnia, the MPs were short people. "You can take him," Sergeant First Class Green said. I was in great shape, and they knew I liked to fire the weapons at the range and that I was good at it—especially the Mark 19 grenade launcher, which is belt fed and fully automatic and can push out about 350 40 mm rounds per minute. It has a butterfly trigger in the back, and when you squeeze it, it just keeps going. It's extremely heavy, so it's mounted to the top of the vehicle, and it takes two guys to put it up. It can do a lot of damage—we could take out a building with it—but it was also fun to shoot at the range. Out on patrol, they made me the gunner.

Green was my platoon sergeant, but he was also an MP, so he pushed me to do more.

We provided security for the 1.3 million Bosnian refugees trying to get back home. At some point during our deployment, the mission changed from implementation to stabilization, so the US military oversaw mine removal and inspected weapons sites, as well as watching the zone of separation to make sure the different factions didn't meet and kill each other. The Muslims often tried to return to their former homes in the Serbian areas, and the Serbs were all too happy to meet them—and shoot them. We also had to keep people out of minefields.

It was incredibly cold. In Sarajevo, it doesn't top 65 degrees Fahrenheit often, even in August. By September, it was dipping into the 40s. It rained. It snowed. It fogged. In December, the temperature hovered at or below freezing. We knew the locals often didn't have heat as they worked to rebuild after the destruction of the war.

At first, we lived in tents, which meant we got to know one another well. When we weren't working, we had the kerosene heater going with hot cocoa, and we played cards—spades, of course. People don't realize that soldiers do everything together.

A buddy even stood guard while I took a shower. So, like a family, we had to figure out how to get along.

We shared everything, from electronics to music and books, partially because everybody was bored when they were not working but also for the shared experience of it. It gave us something else to talk about. I read my first book in English on that deployment—*A Time to Kill*, by John Grisham. I loved it. I started to read everything he wrote.

Eventually, as one battalion moved out, we moved into their Conex shelters. Each shelter had six or eight bunk beds, so we were still all jammed in together.

I soldiered twenty-four seven for nine months. I loved how much I was learning, loved the people I worked with, loved that I felt as if I was putting good out into the world.

I cleaned my weapon constantly. I exercised a lot. We had to figure out how to get from point A to point B while following all the rules of a convoy. We conducted risk assessments—learning how to avoid land mines by staying in the middle of the road and thinking about who would take the lead if something happened. Luckily, nothing happened to us.

I also learned not to hit any cows.

That may seem obvious, as a cow could do a decent amount of damage to a truck and nobody wants to clean up that kind of mess. But for a local farmer? That cow could have been his entire life. It could have provided the majority of his family's sustenance. It could have provided the cheese he sold in the market. And he could be compensated for that cow, but it would be bureaucratic bullshit time away from the things he needed to be doing, like tending fields or taking care of chickens or rebuilding tractors or whatever. If we killed his cow, he was going to be pissed, and pissed-off locals are never good for soldiers.

At night, after a day of not hitting mines or cows, we'd have a hot meal, and hot meals mean a lot to a soldier. It was cold outside, and we maybe had MRE spaghetti out of a plastic pouch for breakfast. And lunch was from the rest of the MRE, whatever we could fit in our pockets that wasn't pork so Jewish and Muslim soldiers couldn't eat it. Hot meals were a big deal.

But, after patrol, I still had to do my admin job. If we came in late from patrol, the other soldiers were set: their platoon sergeant would make sure somebody saved a plate for them for when they got back. I was not part of those platoons. I was on my own.

Except for Sergeant First Class Green: he made sure I had a hot dinner. He acted as my platoon sergeant, my supervisor, my older brother. At Christmas, people sent a bunch of care packages. I'm a guy who doesn't celebrate Christmas, but he made sure I had one—some comfort from home in the form of socks and snacks.

Sergeant Green—the way he looked out for me—was a lesson in and of itself. I wanted to be that kind of NCO (noncommissioned officer).

He knew I wasn't getting a lot of sleep, because I started taking classes at the University of Maryland while I was in Bosnia, too: English and the history of Western civilization.

But I was also trying to figure out what I was seeing in Bosnia—it wasn't like anything I had seen in Egypt.

It was nuts: I lived in a cold tent because Christians had been killing Muslims because of their religion. But when I asked the local Muslims about their religion, they didn't know much about it. People weren't extremists there. In fact, they were what we called "Muslim light." So they were sort of culturally Muslim but not practicing. Men and women mixed freely. If a girl wanted to flirt with a guy, she didn't think twice about it, and neither did anybody else. Many of the Bosnians had never fasted in their lives. They were more defined by their culture.

That may not seem to make a lot of sense, but you see it a lot in the United States: Jews who say they're culturally religious—they know the stories and light the candles, but they don't necessarily believe the Torah is the word of God. Or you'll see Christians who put up a tree and color Easter eggs but who don't necessarily believe that there was a virgin birth or that Jesus rose from the dead. Jews who ask for forgiveness on Yom Kippur but eat shrimp the rest of the year. Christians who go to church on Christmas, and that's it. I'm not judging—I've been known to have a beer or two. People like their traditions, and they like to raise their children in a community. In any case, these Bosnians called themselves Muslims, but when I asked them about Ramadan, they said, "Yeah, I've heard of it."

After years of "that's haram," that seemed like a pretty neat version of Islam.

All of these differences inspired questions. I liked to read Islamic lectures—I had been brought up doing that—as well as books about Islam. Just like Christianity, there are some great stories there. Of course, some of them are the same stories; just like Christianity and Judaism, Islam has its roots in the Old Testament. Muslims consider Christ a prophet, rather than the son of God, and Muhammad is an additional prophet, albeit the most important one for Islam. Essentially, Muhammad said we had fallen away from God's intent—the things we had learned from Moses and Adam and Abraham and Jesus—and we needed to do things better. The Quran provides the teachings Muhammad said he received verbatim from God. It incorporates Arabic culture, as well as addressing some of the problems in the Arabic world at the time, such as tithing the rich to make sure everyone had a minimum income or condemning female infanticide.

But as I read my lectures surrounded by "Muslim light" in Bosnia, I started to notice some cultural differences in the Islam of other countries. One book went like this: If you do this, you're going to hell. If you do that, you're going to hell. After you die, there will be a snake in your grave, and the snake will bite you in the fucking ass every day for the rest of eternity.

Sweet.

It did, in fact, sound as if hell would suck. But everything in that book and in many others like it was based on total fear. That's not what I remember growing up. I started paying attention to where books like that were published.

Saudi Arabia.

Saudi Arabia.

Saudi Arabia.

Every time I read a book that featured this version of extreme Islam, it had been published in Saudi Arabia.

I stopped buying books that had been published in Saudi Arabia.

Aden Ayro? He nursed on them. He represented everything that, even as a young soldier, I knew was bad.

I'd seen some differences even on base back in Texas. There

was a guy at Fort Hood—an African American Muslim guy—who insisted that he couldn't shave his beard because of his religion.

"Islam does not say you have to grow your beard," the imam at our mosque told him.

"But this is part of my identity," the guy said. He had converted while he was in the military, and somebody—some street imam—told him that for people to know he was a Muslim, he couldn't shave. I remember thinking, *Why are you doing this? Why does anyone else need to know your religion?* As a convert, he took bits and pieces of what he was told by whoever was talking.

In Bosnia, they embraced a cultural identity, which also included bits and pieces of Islam.

One day, we provided security, as we had done before, for a United Nations team as it investigated a potential genocide site. We walked into a warehouse, daylight shining in through windows with no panes, but it still felt cold and dark. Silent. Concrete floor. Pipes running overhead. Bullet holes in the wall.

You could tell whether the victim had been a child or an adult by the height of the hole. The investigators had chemicals that changed color depending on what material they came into contact with. Blood. Brain cells.

It took years to investigate the genocide because the Bosnian Serbs conducted a coordinated cover-up of things like mass graves by using backhoes to dig them up and move them far away from where people were killed. US intelligence later found those graves using satellite imagery. They then used DNA testing to identify people. The investigators gathered eyewitness accounts, talked to relatives about their missing family members, and interviewed people involved in the attacks. They also visited detention areas where the Serbs said they were holding the Bosniaks. There was no one there.

I thought a lot about what happened there.

The only crime these people committed was being born where they were and having Muslim parents. That's not even a choice—in most cases, people inherit their religions just as they do the color of their eyes. That's particularly the case in a place where there is no freedom to think, such as Yugoslavia, which was a communist country. There was no room to explore what you believe.

At that point, we weren't thinking about the possibility that Bosnian Muslims could become radicalized, just as I had seen happen in my youth in Egypt. But Muslims from around the world read that Muslim women had been raped and that men and children had been killed. The Bosniaks already received financial aid from Saudi Arabia and Iran. Long before the Americans got there, the Mujahideen began to arrive from Afghanistan, Iran, Egypt, and other Arab countries to help the Bosniaks.

When we left Bosnia, the Saudis came in and said, "Hey. We're here to help you learn about Islam. We'll build you some mosques. You're our Muslim brothers." And they taught them radical Islam. In Bosnia, as well as in Kosovo, the locals looked at the Saudis and thought, *These guys must be very good Muslims. Mecca is in Saudi Arabia. Prophet Muhammad is from Saudi Arabia. The Quran is from Saudi Arabia. They must know what they're doing.* They lived in the aftermath of a war zone, and it was a hostile environment with mines and booby traps—the Serbs left explosives everywhere, from sweatshirts on the side of the road to dishes in an abandoned house. When the Saudis came in offering comfort and pride, the local Muslims listened.

Every time we leave a gap—either by ignoring a place or by going in and then leaving—someone else will fill that gap. Years later, in Iraq, I would encounter Bosnians who had come to fight with the extremists.

The mission itself? I think we had that right.

In September, we stepped up patrols for national elections—and we guarded polling places and escorted ballots.

Many of the Bosnian Muslims had fled to Germany, and they came back to vote, so we escorted them. And then we escorted their buses back so they would be safe.

I thought back to my friends and family who had told me that joining the military was haram. I knew the world was watching—particularly the Arab world—and I was proud of what my friends were learning about my military and my new family.

Which is good because it was some pretty miserable shit. We started each day at four or five o'clock in the morning, and we sometimes worked past midnight. As we escorted the buses so people could vote, it rained. And rained. It was that cold rain that seeps into your bones until you feel like you'll never be warm again, so it was miserable for us, and it was miserable for them.

But as I looked around, the soldiers and the Muslim Bosnians all looked happy and excited. They were doing it. They were part of something big. Nobody complained about the rain. Nobody complained about the cold. Nobody complained about being hungry. As people voted, we secured the area for them. We saw children playing in the gray. They reacted to our energy, and we to theirs.

I could see who I was helping. I wanted to do it in a bigger way. If I needed to fight, I wanted to see whom I was fighting— not fight by pushing paperwork across a desk. I wanted to see the impact of what I was doing. It wasn't a video game. It wasn't a briefing in a clean room with a big table and a bunch of maps. It wasn't video images watched from a distance. When you can see the consequences of your actions, good and bad, it has profound meaning.

As I sat there in the rain watching children play, I knew it was time to make a change.

First, I'd have to pay my dues.

ON AUGUST 7, 1998, terrorists bombed the American embassies in Kenya and Tanzania. Muslim terrorists.

Friday morning. August. It should have been a day of rushing through work, buffing hallway floors and emptying trash cans, and then rushing out of the office before someone thought up some bullshit duty to ruin the weekend.

Instead, my heart once again dropped.

Please don't let it be a Muslim terrorist.

Please let there be few casualties.

Soon, Armed Forces Network's television broadcasts showed nothing but buildings reduced to heaps of rubble and grim-faced rescue workers searching for any hint of survivors.

This time, the terrorists killed Muslims in Africa—home. The people at the embassies were just people going to work—cooks and clerks and cleaners, in addition to the Americans serving there. They killed more than two hundred people, including twelve Americans, and more than four thousand were injured. Brown people. Black people. White people. My people from both of my homes.

As I watched the news, all I could think was that these guys used my religion to justify a massacre of mostly poor Muslims and Christians in those countries. I was devastated. I knew that, once again, it would reflect on all of us.

I had no idea I would spend the majority of my career hunting down the people who bombed the embassies, as well as those who inspired them.

After being in Bosnia, I had wanted to see more of the world. I called my branch manager, who said a spot in Germany was opening up. I returned to Fort Hood from Bosnia in April 1997, and by July, I was in a "welcome" class in Würzburg learning how to say, "Ein kleines Bier, bitte"—a phrase no one ever used. I was based at a tiny post with a military intelligence unit and the First Infantry Division headquarters.

I enjoyed Germany. For a young soldier, it was pretty self-contained: We did PT. We went to work. We went to the barracks. We went to the gym again. There were four of us who hung out all the time—two white guys, a Black guy, and me. There were times when we went to the club and they wouldn't let the Black guy in, and that pissed us all off, but generally, we danced and had fun. We ran in vineyards and local parks and enjoyed nature. We took trips to Amsterdam, France, and Vienna. My friends and I had a great time.

But after the attacks, our lives shifted: We couldn't go to the clubs. Our German friends couldn't come on base. We pulled guard shifts to keep ourselves and the military families safe.

At the time, I went to a mosque—really just a room—at a university near base. Some of the guys looked like extremists, but back then, we didn't see people differently: a guy with a big beard was just a guy with a big beard. But at the mosque, I learned that some dude named Osama bin Laden had issued a fatwa: $10,000 for each soldier killed.

Bin Laden's dad was a Saudi multimillionaire—the wealthiest nonroyal Saudi—originally from Yemen, and his mom came from a secular Syrian family, back when Syria felt pretty westernized. In 1979, bin Laden joined the Mujahideen forces fighting the Soviet Union in Afghanistan. By 1988, he had formed al-Qaeda, and by 1992, he had been banned from Saudi Arabia and started operating out of Sudan—too damned close to home for me. The United States put pressure on Sudan, and by 1996, bin Laden had moved to Afghanistan. That's when he declared war on the United States.

And issued his bullshit fatwa.

I was a guy in a uniform going to a mosque to pray. I needed to rethink that for my own safety, which made me angry. Here I was serving in the US Army, and I had just come back from helping Muslims in another country who had been persecuted for their beliefs, and I needed to worry about some jackass in Afghanistan keeping me from going to the mosque.

On top of that, I felt judged because I was a Muslim, even as I was angered by how these terrorists made Islam look. In the Quran, it says, "Whoever kills an innocent person, it is as though he has killed all mankind. And whoever saves a life, it is as though he has saved all mankind" (5:32). Nothing about Muslims or Christians. "All mankind." I'm a Muslim, but I'm as good as anyone else. I served for all.

The attack would only make things worse.

I worked in the NBC (nuclear, biological, chemical) section directly for a sergeant major and a lieutenant colonel—top-heavy, but that's normal for an admin job.

The lieutenant colonel was one of those guys who don't want any drama and so don't address the drama, which means the drama increases. Nice enough, but weak.

During Ramadan, I learned the sergeant major was something else altogether.

Our division commander sent out a memo saying Muslim soldiers should be exempted from physical training because they were fasting. I thought it was cool that the division commander cared enough about his Muslim troops to send out a note.

I went ahead and did PT anyway. I would spend the day hungry, but I thought of it as a way to enhance the mind-body piece of fasting: to think about the important things, to be grateful for what a normal day looked like, to learn more about what I was capable of.

As we warmed up, we got ready to do a ski-jumper exercise— basically a squat jump that moves from side to side.

"Gamal is incapable of performing the ski-jumper exercise," the sergeant major said. "He's just another camel jockey."

This time, I knew what it meant.

The nice but weak lieutenant colonel heard him and said nothing.

The memo from the division commander also said soldiers fasting for Ramadan should be released early so they could break their fasts after not eating all day.

The sergeant major kept me until after dark.

"Hey," my admin supervisor said, "my corporal's fasting."

"I don't fucking care," the sergeant major said.

At work, he had me type up his college papers. At festivals, he wore his uniform in his wife's booth so soldiers would feel "inspired" to buy from her. And every damned day, after deciding I should be his driver, he had me wash our ugly green VW van—whether we had used it or not.

One day, as I drove him around, we passed a big sign advertising Delta Force. Delta Force is, of course, the First Special Forces Operational Detachment–Delta, ███████████████████████ ██ ██ ████████████████████████. I didn't know yet exactly what any of that meant, but I knew they were badass.

"You should go to this briefing," the sergeant major said.

I perked up. I thought he meant it.

"You think I'm good enough to be in Delta Force?"

"Yeah, man," he said, "they can always use a terrorist."

Who even says that shit? Here I was, still in my twenties, enamored by the Army and all I was learning, and here's this opportunity for this guy to teach me—to help me love the Army more. To help me be a great soldier.

I did go to that briefing. I had realized in Bosnia I didn't want to be an admin guy and sit behind a desk. I wanted to go to Ranger school, and I wanted to do all of the Army things.

But I wasn't a US citizen. Bolo.

I didn't tell him.

Every problem has a solution. This, I already knew.

First, I tried to figure out what the dude's issue was. It appeared that the sergeant major was a racist fuckup with a chip on his shoulder.

Swell.

There did not appear to be a way to smooth that over. But if he'd gotten to know me, rather than continually berating me, he would have learned I had a background in law. I spent my downtime learning the Army regulations I would need to make sure he couldn't make anyone else's life a living hell.

For six months, I kept track of everything. On a floppy disk. I was going to use my admin-guy superpowers for good.

I got smart about a lot of things: I researched conflict of interest. I looked up misuse of government property. I checked into formal versus informal equal opportunity (EO) complaints and the amount of time the commander had to determine whether a formal complaint was substantiated—and then what happened next if it was.

In the meantime, because I wasn't going to let the NBC sergeant major hold me back, I called my admin supervisor and said, "I want to go to the E5 board"—the board to be promoted to sergeant. In Bosnia, I had been promoted to specialist, and I wore that rank for about two weeks before they promoted me to corporal, which meant I had the responsibilities of a sergeant.

"You're not ready yet," he said. "You've only been in the Army for two years."

"Send me," I said.

By then, my English had improved, so I started competing in boards, which meant I stood before a panel of my leadership while they drilled me about everything from marching to weapons and unit history. Memorizing my Smart Book in basic had been good training: I kept winning. Soldier of the Month. Soldier of the Quarter.

Before the boards, I had already made a bit of a name for myself at the battalion level by virtue of my smart-ass, competitive nature.

I had gotten sick early on, and the doctors gave me a strong antibiotic. I felt weak as hell, but I went ahead and did PT. Slowly. So the battalion sergeant major—not the sergeant major I worked for—and the nice but weak lieutenant colonel pulled me aside.

"You're in your twenties," they told me. "There's no reason for you to be running slower than we are."

I knew I was much faster than they were, and if they had spent any time looking at my record, they would have known that, too.

"Hey, if you can beat me in a run, I'll give you a four-day pass," the lieutenant colonel said.

"Every time I beat you?" I asked. "Or just if I beat you once."

"Every time," he said, thinking there was no way I would beat him ever.

"Okay, sir, if I beat you next week on Thursday, can I have next weekend off?"

"Absolutely," he said.

I didn't just beat him—I beat everybody.

He gave me one four-day pass. And then he said, "That shit's not going to happen again."

The battalion sergeant major presided over the E5 (sergeant) board. He was Hispanic, so I looked at him and thought, *I can do that one day.* He knew that I was doing the job of a sergeant and that I kept winning the board competitions, so he asked when I was going to go to the E5 board.

"Sergeant major, ask my supervisor," I said.

He made sure the racist sergeant major sent me to the board, even though he didn't want to. I went the following month.

After I went to the E5 board and proved myself, I met with my company equal opportunity representative, who was a friend of the NBC sergeant major.

"You can come back after lunch," she said, obviously brushing me off.

I went to the first sergeant, who was from Guam. Technically, the sergeant major outranked the first sergeant, but the first sergeant was still top of the enlisted chain in the company.

In his mind, I was a good soldier. I'd done well at the boards. I was a good runner. I didn't drink. I didn't party. I didn't take drugs. I was squeaky clean.

"First sergeant," I said, "can I use your open-door policy?"

He probably knew what was coming. He may have been looking for a reason to get rid of dead weight. I told him the details.

"I saved everything on a floppy disk," I said.

He called in the company commander.

"I went to the equal opportunity rep," I said. "She brushed me off. If you guys are planning to do the same, I'm going to email every Congress member I can think of."

"You don't need to do that," they said.

It does say something about the process that I felt as if I had to. I knew that the system failed a lot of people—that women dealing with assault or harassment had to talk about why they wore what they wore, why they went out by themselves, or why they continued to work for men they accused of rape even after filing a complaint. That lower-enlisted soldiers had no recourse if they filed a complaint against their bosses and the chain of command did nothing. That the good ol' boy network kept cases from proceeding.

That if the system worked properly, the racist sergeant major would never have grown up to be a racist sergeant major.

But my leadership told me to go finish my lunch and asked me not to go back to the office right away. While I was gone, they told the weak lieutenant colonel and the racist sergeant major that I had filed a formal complaint and that they would support me.

When I think about how a company commander, with the full support of his first sergeant, within hours, said, "I'm going to use my command authority to initiate an investigation" against someone who outranked him, it strikes me as profound. But as I was a recent immigrant, it also gave me some belief that I was in a place where I could own my dreams. As a corporal, I could push forward a case for equity.

At the battalion level, they appointed an Asian American lieutenant colonel to look into my case. "I'm a minority, just like you," he said. "Tell me what happened." I felt like the system was going to take care of me. The way my leadership handled it sticks with me to this day. I wanted to grow up to be that kind of leader.

By that point, as a male minority, I did understand the game a little better. I was surrounded by successful minority soldiers, including women, and I watched how my leaders achieved past the stereotypes.

If someone else put in four hours, I put in eight. If someone else could run two miles in twelve minutes, I did it in eleven. If someone else had a college degree, I got a master's degree. If someone else had a master's degree, I got two.

The system says, "Get educated. Get points for physical fitness. Get points for boards. Get promoted."

If you're different, you have to go above and beyond everybody else just to look like everybody else. And if you tell me I got where I am because of affirmative action, I'm going to take my awards and accomplishments and I'm going to shove them right up your ass.

After my complaint, they did end up moving me. I worked for Major General David Grange, who was the division commander. He had served with the 101st in Vietnam and with other Army Special Operations Forces (SOF) units in Grenada, and he was a deputy commander in 1991's Desert Storm.

I learned everything I could from him and Colonel Carter Ham, who was our operations officer before becoming chief of staff of the division. He pinned my E5 rank. He started as an enlisted soldier but later became the division commander.

Once, we were in the field, and some guys came to clean the porta-potty.

"What do you think of that smell?" Colonel Ham asked.

"Sir, it smells like shit," I said.

"No, it doesn't," Colonel Ham said. "It smells like money. You know how much these guys are getting paid for a job that nobody else wants to do?"

After I retired, I thought about that advice. It still gives a competitive edge to my business.

(I don't clean porta-potties. But I do what others are afraid to do.)

"You should reclass as military intelligence," Ham said one day as we ran together.

"I'm not an American citizen yet," I said.

Back then, you had to serve for three years before you could get your citizenship. The instant I was eligible, my leadership helped me with my paperwork and then sent me back to the United States to take my citizenship test.

In the States, after I passed my citizenship exam, the immigration officer threw away my green card (it was really pink). "You no longer need anything to prove you're an American," the guy said. "What are you going to do?"

"Well," I said. "I'm going to be all that I can be."

That was the Army motto at the time, and cheesy as it may sound, I had embraced it full force. Immigration swore me in early because I was in the military. I got my letter from President Bill Clinton. And I flew back to Germany feeling like a different person.

I immediately applied for my clearance.

After I got it, a woman named Sergeant First Class Pringle offered me a position teaching Arabic at the Defense Language Institute—a dream job for any thinking person. A gig in California? Sweet.

"No," I said. "I want to go to Fort Bragg."

"You must be the dumbest person in the Army," she said.

ELEVEN   THE WOMEN ARE THE ONES WHO WEAVE THE PATTERN

A FIRST LIEUTENANT LED our convoy—the first into Kosovo in 1999. He was young, inexperienced, and supermotivated.

You know where this is going.

There were about 120 of us. I drove the second-to-last Humvee, along with two other sergeants. One of them, Sergeant M., was Ranger qualified and generally awesome.

It felt as if we had been driving for far too long, and the sun was in the wrong place.

"Hey, Ranger," I said to Sergeant M., "don't you feel as if we might be going in the wrong direction?"

It was another battle between Christians and Muslims. This time it was the majority–Orthodox Christian Serbians against the majority-Muslim ethnic Albanians in Kosovo.

After World War II, Kosovo—like Bosnia-Herzegovina—had become part of Yugoslavia, along with Serbia. Kosovo was a province of Serbia. Kosovo wanted autonomy, and the Kosovo Liberation Army (KLA) started fighting for it. After another massacre, this time of sixty Muslims, including eighteen women and ten children, the United Nations and Russia brokered a peace, but it failed. The KLA attacked civilians in Kosovo, and the Yugoslavs and Serbs began to kill Muslims. They killed hundreds of people, as well as destroying homes and mosques, until eight hundred thousand people fled the region. NATO forces bombed military targets, there was another peace agreement, and there we were, as peacekeepers, following a lieutenant into Kosovo.

"We gotta follow him," Sergeant M. said. "Even if he's wrong. That's how it works."

The LT was a nice enough guy—we had no beef with him—and we didn't want to embarrass him by calling him out on the radio.

Instead, we asked for a piss break.

"Piss in your bottle," he said. "We can't be late."

Sergeant M. smiled at me from the passenger's seat.

Definitely lost.

Twenty minutes later, we saw a sign: "Welcome to Greece."

"It appears," Sergeant M. said, "that we have missed a turn."

By the time we arrived in Kosovo—after turning the entire convoy around—darkness had set and rain had started to pour. We still needed to set up tents.

That marked the beginning of my second deployment. Our company would set the foundation for what is now known as Camp Bondsteel, which serves as NATO headquarters for the continuing mission there. But that night, I slept with four other dudes in a hot, humid one-man tent. We would not shower for another thirty days.

In Kosovo, I did my usual thing: patrolled, studied, learned, exercised, and pushed hard on my badass admin-guy job. Same day, different deployment.

In the meantime, my brother was visiting Alexandria and thought it was time for me to settle down. We weren't necessarily on the same page about this: I was doing just fine on my own stationed in Germany, thanks. No hurry.

But . . . he met this girl. Her family was friends with my family in Egypt. Egypt, of course, is what I had been trying to get away from: no way was I going to go start a family back home.

"I found somebody for you," my brother said. "You really have to call her."

"Man, I'm in Kosovo," I said. "I'm in a war zone, and you want me to call a girl back home."

"You've got to meet her," he said.

"Man, I'm not interested," I said. "I'm busy. I'm not interested in anything."

"Hold on," he said. He connected her through.

I fell in love with her voice. She was sweet from day one.

My brother, of course, knew my taste in women. She's really cute, of course. And I wanted someone who had a similar background, who had black hair, who was smart, who was from Alexandria, who was willing to travel around the world with me, who would wait for me when I deployed, and who was short like me.

It was a big list.

I kept calling her. We talked a lot; my phone bill was extremely high. She had lived in Algeria for a while as a child, and then she went to Egypt for high school and college. I have no doubt that she is smarter than I am. And she is levelheaded—I realized early that she would keep me grounded.

After my deployment ended, I took leave and went to Egypt. Two months after that—after I moved to Fort Bragg—she visited her uncle in Pennsylvania, so I headed to Pennsylvania, too. I asked her a lot of questions, just throwing things out there to see if our futures could line up.

"I don't want to buy a house in Egypt," I said. "I don't want to live in Egypt."

"Yeah, me either," she said.

I liked to talk, and she liked to listen. And it drives me crazy when someone speaks half English, half Arabic. Pick one. I spoke to her only in Arabic. After a month, she said, "Do you speak English?"

Everything matched—everything fit.

I asked her to marry me. Of all the decisions I've made, she was the best one.

TWELVE
THE ALL-AMERICAN DREAM

INSTEAD OF FORT BRAGG, North Carolina, I found myself exactly where I had started: down the street from the same Manhattan deli I'd worked at when I lived in New Jersey. This time, five or six years later, they gave me an access badge to FBI headquarters.

It was even better than when Sergeant Green gave me a laptop.

Blue badge, full access. I was over the clouds every day walking through those glass front doors at Federal Plaza.

It wasn't where I expected to be, but the operations sergeant major in my new unit at Fort Bragg also ran fast and long—so we ran together. He liked to chat about what was going on in the unit, so I learned a lot about how things work and how to lead. Sergeant Major Washington was fit, a great jumpmaster, and always calm. He was an awesome mentor. One morning, on a run, he told me the FBI needed people to translate some sensitive documents. This was in 2000.

The unit wanted to send a guy named Mohammed—the only guy in the brigade who spoke Arabic, the sergeant major told me as we ran. But Mohammed did not know any Arabic. He just had an Arabic-sounding name. My name sounded Spanish because of the screwup on my green card, so he didn't know I was from Egypt.

But the admin officer knew.

"Your running buddy speaks Arabic," he told Sergeant Major Washington.

"How the fuck do you know Arabic?" Sergeant Major Washington asked me.

"I was born speaking Arabic, Sergeant Major."

"I thought you were fucking Puerto Rican."

"No, I'm fucking Egyptian, Sergeant Major," I said.

Of course, my new wife had just arrived in the United States.

She didn't know a soul. And Fort Bragg is ugly. Strip malls. Strip clubs. Laundromats. Pawn shops. She had come from a safe place where she had friends and her own interests, but we were out in the middle of nowhere with our little house and our little porch.

Someone stole our bikes right off that little porch. That scared her, and it should have, because who does that to their neighbors? Worse, who does that to their coworkers?

Just after she arrived, they asked me to take that temporary FBI assignment.

Police in Manchester, England, had found a manual while searching an al-Qaeda member's home. The dude had it on his computer in a folder called something like "Military Stuff: Call to Jihad." He may as well have called it "Dear Cops: Here's What You're Looking For."

I like to think that, if Allah were to choose people to fight for the Islamist cause, he'd pick smart people. But like most religious wars, it's about power, not religion, and Allah does not appear to be involved.

In any case, the Justice Department planned to use the manual as evidence in the trials of two men charged in those embassy bombings that had happened in Kenya and Tanzania—the ones that happened while I was in Germany.

At that point, we didn't know exactly what the job would be, but my wife and I talked about the possibilities: "This is really important. It's good for the United States, and it's going to be good for us." We went back and forth.

"Go," she said. "Let's do this."

She's stronger than I am. Three weeks after she arrived in the United States, I left her by herself for three months. Fortunately, my friends and their wives quickly took her in.

In New York, we worked in cubicles on a big, open floor—tons of people working there. The FBI had brought in four of us: an Army woman; an Army guy; an Air Force guy, a nice, classy guy; and me. I was the only native speaker. For the first couple of days, they gave us some tasks to work on. Then, about two days in, they gave us this huge manual.

"It's the al-Qaeda manual," they told us. "You guys need to translate this before you go back to your military jobs."

At first, we thought it was going to take forever. But then we started flipping through it.

"Man, this is going to be the easiest thing ever," I said, a few pages in.

Half of it came from US Army field manuals—even the little pictures and graphics were in there. Between memorizing the Smart Book in basic training and preparing for all those boards, I could recite a lot of it by heart.

We thought it came from an Egyptian American kid who had worked as a supply clerk in the US military. He stole a bunch of manuals—most of this stuff is online now—and translated it into Arabic. He copied things like how to seize an airfield, how to read a map, how to set up an ambush.

That shows you how naive we were—that we allowed people easy access to things they could use against us.

But some of the manual also looked like this:

Islamic governments have never and will never be established through peaceful solutions and cooperative councils. They are established as they [always] have been

by pen and gun

by word and bullet

by tongue and teeth

I don't know what those fuckers were doing with their tongues, but it's not anything I remember from the Quran.

The manual also contained some messed-up, scary shit, like this:

MISSIONS REQUIRED OF THE MILITARY ORGANIZATION:
The main mission for which the Military Organization is responsible is:

The overthrow of the godless regimes and their replacement with an Islamic regime.

Other missions consist of the following:

1. Gathering information about the enemy, the land, the installations, and the neighbors.

2. Kidnaping enemy personnel, documents, secrets, and arms.

3. Assassinating enemy personnel as well as foreign tourists.

4. Freeing the brothers who are captured by the enemy.

5. Spreading rumors and writing statements that instigate people against the enemy.

6. Blasting and destroying the places of amusement, immorality, and sin; not a vital target.

7. Blasting and destroying the embassies and attacking vital economic centers.

8. Blasting and destroying bridges leading into and out of the cities.

They used the training manual to justify bad behavior, and we found out years later, in Iraq and elsewhere, that it was an effective brainwashing tool for new recruits to the terrorist organization. They offered reasoning for why beating someone is okay as a means to get information, as well as justification for killing people who withheld information. They found "scripture" that allowed exchanging hostages for money.

Not my Islam. Not the majority's Islam. Most Muslims—in the States and around the world—were horrified when word got out about the manual.

I worked with a guy who tested new people coming in to see if their Arabic skills were good enough to work for the FBI. He was a seventy-something-year-old Egyptian guy. Christian. He had been working, for a couple of years, on a translation of the Quran into English.

"You know I can go buy you one at the shop down the street for twenty dollars?" I said.

"Yeah, but it won't have the same nuances," he said. I don't imagine that it would.

One day, he asked me to cover for him because he was going to go test new applicants. When he came back, he said one had passed and one had failed—two Egyptian Americans.

"Let me guess which one passed and which one failed," I said. "Tell me their names."

He told me. I told him who passed and who failed.

"How did you know?" he asked.

"Because the one who passed has a Christian name and the one who failed has a Muslim name," I said. In the Middle East, you can tell by a person's name if they're Christian or Muslim—or if they're Sunni or Shia or Kurdish.

"No, no, no," he said, "we don't do that."

But there were about ten native Arabic speakers at FBI headquarters, and all but one of them were Christians. The one Muslim guy had Americanized his name so you couldn't tell what flavor of Arab he was.

"That's a flaw in your system," I told the translator of the Quran. "The population in the Arab world is like ninety percent Muslim and ten percent Christian. If you're hiring from that community, that should be reflected. At least seven of the Arabic speakers here should be Muslim."

I asked the Quran translator what, exactly, he tested people on. Poetry. Literature. Proverbs.

"This is justification for you to fail people," I said. "If I were going to test someone's Arabic, I would talk to them on the phone for five minutes. You've been doing this job for twenty years. How often do your people translate poetry?"

This will surprise no one: We weren't translating Nobel Prize winners. We were usually translating something a dumbass had written for another dumbass. If they were smart people, they wouldn't have joined a cult.

They had so few Muslim agents, and so very few Muslim linguists, that they were fighting an enemy they didn't know. We should have been inside the enemies' minds. We should have been learning their tactics. It was spelled out in the documents.

Three or four FBI agents did solid work. But they didn't work with agents in other departments. In fact, they were on their own separate floor, so no one talked to the translators about things they picked up as they translated.

There was also no sense of urgency. The government had sat on that manual for two or three years before we got there and only began to translate it because they needed it for the embassy trials.

I can't say any of us could have predicted what was coming. We wouldn't have seen it. But looking back?

Damn. We were so fucking stupid.

Everything changed after 9/11. After that, they had an office filled with sharp, dedicated professionals, including many Muslims. This was a huge shift, and they were phenomenal. As far as patriotism goes? The Muslim agents wore their flags on their chests. They took the attacks personally: people from my religion did this, and I owe it to my country to work hard.

After we finished translating, Sergeant First Class Pringle called again to ask if I wanted to reclassify from my administrative job to 98 Golf—or "cryptic linguist."

I wanted to be an interrogator, but the Army didn't see a need for an Arabic interrogator. While it's ironic, it's probably the best thing that ever happened to my career—but not because I never worked as an interrogator.

And 98 G meant a $20,000 bonus if I reenlisted. Basically, I'd gather and decipher signal intelligence—SIGINT—or listen in, read, and translate Arabic messages. In the Cold War days, that meant positioning a tracked vehicle where it could catch radio traffic, and then the interpreters would capture messages in Russian and try to crack the code. These were the days before cell phones and armies with laptops.

I went to a base in Texas to learn analysis skills—as well as the tools I needed to process information. I was one of two minority students in both classes and the only student who was a native Arabic speaker. Because I spoke Arabic fluently, they let me do the course at my own pace: "Hey, whenever you're ready for a test, just let us know." It was supposed to be a five-and-a-half-month course, but I finished it in about two and a half months:

A) I grew up speaking Arabic. Hell, I went to law school speaking Arabic.

B) My new wife was waiting for me.

I ended up graduating with the class ahead of me.

From there, I went to airborne school.

In airborne school, they broke everyone down into chalks. On a static line, the lightest guy jumps first—except they usually put an officer first. I was usually the number two guy out of the plane, but in my chalk, the first guy out the door was a chaplain. We went up, and there were like seventy of us in a C-130. Someone always puked, so we were trying to make sure we weren't part of a chain reaction of puking. The jumpmaster told us to, yes, stand up, hook up, and shuffle to the door.

What's a "shuffle"?

We were all supposed to check the equipment of the person in front of us, so I reached up and ran my hand over the chaplain's main parachute, harness, and static line. I tried not to look past him at the ground because while I wasn't terrified, I wasn't exactly comfortable with what I was about to do, and I didn't want to think about it until I did become terrified.

But the chaplain? Ol' boy was saying every prayer he could think of—in between sweating and throwing up.

Oh my god, the smell.

Not gonna throw up; not gonna throw up; not gonna throw up.

I mean, I was scared, but I had it under control.

This happened every single time we jumped out of that plane: the chaplain prayed and sweated and puked.

The third time, I decided to talk to him about it.

"Sir, why are you so worried?" I said. "I mean, if you are scared, I should be terrified, because at least you know that if you die, you're going to heaven. You're a chaplain."

He just looked at me.

"Please just try to calm down a bit because you make me more scared," I said.

And honestly, I had more reason to be scared than he did. His jumps went off without a hitch.

My first jump? I bounced like a Super Ball. I bounced at least five times because I was so light.

Of course, the black hat—that's what we called the instructors— came running over. I figured I was in for some compassion. Maybe he'd even check my vitals to make sure I wasn't dying. Like, "How many fingers am I holding up?" Maybe he'd even ask me if I was all right.

He pulled out his bullhorn.

"November!" he yelled at me. That's what they called trainees who were noncommissioned officers: "November." He had the bullhorn right in my face.

"November!" he screamed. "Did you break your fucking back?"

I couldn't move.

God in heaven, let me die now.

"November! Did you break your fucking back?"

Oh my god, this does not appear to be the good part of dying, with the virgins.

"Did you break your fucking back?"

Jesus fuck, get out of my face.

"Did you break your fucking back?"

He was yelling at me, and I was thinking, *I have to get up. I have to walk.*

I was also thinking, *Oh my god, I think I broke my fucking back.*

I got up.

I had the biggest bruise on my thigh, from my knee to my ass.

"Man, I think you broke it," my roommate said.

"If I can walk, I didn't break it."

I did what the medics always told us to do: I popped some Motrin.

I graduated with my class.

The chaplain?

I don't know why he was so scared on that second jump.

A few years later, in the Unit, I would get to do the free-fall training. In free fall, the lightest guy jumps last.

The low-altitude jumps—like the ones I did with the chaplain—scared me more because we didn't have as much time. If we went wrong, it was too late. Or if the parachute didn't open, it was too late. We were dead. With free fall, we had some time to figure it out.

Or, you know, to panic and piss our pants before we hit the ground.

But in free fall, I also couldn't see anything because the ground was so far away, so it was less scary somehow to jump from higher. With low-altitude jumps, I could see the ground.

If I hit that, it's gonna hurt.

High altitude? It was just dark.

And fun. We'd move at 120 miles per hour. If we were really high up, we had an oxygen tank and a full-face mask. Of course, the Army takes the fun out of everything, so if I had to wear the mask, I couldn't move my head to see anything because I was hooked to a tube that connects to the tank.

In free fall, I had to keep myself symmetrical, or I'd spin. If I moved my body, I would turn in that direction. That meant my equipment had to be perfectly symmetrical, too. The person behind you on a jump is supposed to help with your gear. One time, this guy pulled one strap on my rucksack tight but left the other one loose. It wasn't intentional—I don't know if he forgot or got distracted or what. But when I jumped out, my rucksack was tilted.

I immediately started to spin.

We're not talking about a leisurely spin here. We're talking Gravitron spin—like that carnival ride where they spin you so fast that everyone sticks to the wall and you hope nobody hurls.

Or at least that's how it felt—except I wasn't vertical. I was belly down, and I hadn't just eaten a Coney dog, and I needed to get my shit together so I wouldn't traumatize a suburban family with 2.5 children and a dog by splattering in their backyard.

But nothing worked. I tried arching my back—that's what they trained us to do.

Spin.

I tried holding perfectly still.

Spin.

I tried rotating my body against the spin.

Spin.

Then my oxygen mask started to move. *Great. Now I'm spinning like a top, and I'm about to lose oxygen.*

Hard no.

I brought my arms in from the flailing-turtle position they'd been in to adjust my mask and that stabilized me.

Okay, I'm cool; I'm cool, I thought. *And I'm not going to move again.*

But then I couldn't look at my altimeter—and I had to open my parachute at a certain altitude. If I moved to look, I knew I would start spinning again.

Shit.

But . . . my training kicked in, and I looked to see where everybody else was and what they were doing. I saw other people opening their parachutes. I opened my parachute.

And I lived happily ever after.

My wife made me call her after each jump—even if it was three in the morning. Otherwise, she couldn't sleep. I worked for my country, but she inspired me.

After jump school, I went to the Eighty-Second Airborne Division—the most elite regular Army unit. Dream come true. I made it through all my training, and my wife was there, and things couldn't be better. This—*this*—was what I signed up for.

I was in excellent shape, and it was always fun because people didn't expect much of me because I was small.

But the Eighty-Second had a weird dynamic: 90 percent white guys. My unit had one Black guy—he was supply—and two women. The rest of the unit was just white men. That was much different from my previous unit, and when you're the new guy who sticks out, you pay attention to everyone else who sticks out.

This was important for several reasons, but let me offer two important ones here.

It's hard to move up in the ranks if you're not in infantry or some other field where you're going to get actual combat experience. The

Black guy was supply. Great guy, but he probably wasn't general officer or sergeant major material by virtue of his job keeping him back from the experiences he needed to lead soldiers into combat. Same with the two women.

So, to get more good minority leadership in the military, we need to make sure women and minority soldiers enlist into those hard-skills jobs—or jobs like intelligence—where there is opportunity to move up.

And second, just as I saw at the FBI, the lack of diversity meant a lack of different viewpoints—of ways of looking at the world, of cultural background, and of experiences. That will always be detrimental to a unit and to the nation.

For me, I saw the unit as an opportunity, and it was exactly where I wanted to be. It was a signals intelligence unit. Almost everybody spoke a foreign language, but at that time, everyone was trained in Russian. We were all still thinking Cold War. That had worked out well for us in Desert Storm and not so well for us in Mogadishu, but the Russians were still the enemy, along with China. For training, we'd go out in tracked vehicles, we'd set up some antennas, and we'd listen in, translate, and send along messages. The people in that unit were great—supersmart. They liked to read. They liked to talk about foreign affairs. They listened to NPR. There was a guy from Los Angeles who was into salsa dancing, and everybody would drink tequila and smoke cigars and talk about the world's problems.

It was a bit different from being an admin clerk.

I thought I had made it.

MY FIRST SERGEANT TOLD me I should go to a briefing. Our unit had received an invitation for a secretive unit. "You'll like it," he told me. I had no idea what it was for—I mean, the name of the Unit is classified, so the last thing they're going to do is send out a memo like, "Hey, at 10:00 a.m. Monday, we're going to tell you everything there is to know about the Unit." It wouldn't have mattered—I had never heard of the Unit before. Top said go, so I went.

During the recruitment briefing, they didn't say anything, really, for the first ten minutes—at least, not enough for us to know what the hell was going on. Then they said, "We can't tell you who we are. We can't tell you what you'll be doing. If you're interested, stay in the room. If you're not, leave."

About half the people left. They did not want to take that leap of faith. The recruiters didn't say anything to make me stay or leave, so I stayed. After the others left, a recruiter interviewed me—he asked a whole bunch of weird questions: philosophical questions, questions about what I saw as the biggest problems in the world, questions about what I liked to read.

The recruiter told me he didn't know what I could do—what I was capable of. He couldn't tell me what my chances were. He told me that selection would push me further than I'd ever been pushed and that it might be helpful to me on an individual level. He couldn't tell me what my job would be or what the missions might look like.

"But will we—"

"We cannot tell you."

They wanted people who were willing to take a risk without knowing the prize.

Guys who came for the money? They were not the right people.

The best people—the right people—wanted to make an impact and believed in the mission. They were crazy enough to try something new to make it happen. They cared.

But I wasn't there yet.

I told the recruiter I had a packet in for officer candidate school—but also that my wife was pregnant and that I was thinking it was time to get out altogether and try something new. I had paid my debt. Nobody saw a need for an Arabic linguist. It was time to roll.

I put the packet from the recruiter in the trunk of my car and didn't think about it again.

By 2001, I felt frustrated. I still loved the people I worked with, but I felt as if I was hitting a plateau as far as my career went. Nobody seemed excited about Arabic speakers, even with the known al-Qaeda threat. Bin Laden had formed the organization in 1988, and in 1995, a man arrested in the Philippines said the terrorist group planned to crash a plane into a US federal building.

In 1993, men connected to al-Qaeda bombed the World Trade Center. Then came the attacks on the American embassies in Tanzania and Kenya. Somalia's warlord Mohamed Farrah Aidid—the guy who sparked the battle depicted in *Black Hawk Down*—was so worried about the Muslim Brotherhood that he created his own extremist religious organization as a propaganda measure to counter it. Still, it seemed as if American officials had filled their ears with cotton. In 1999, our own people said, in a federal study on terrorism, that al-Qaeda was our biggest threat (just as today, our own people say white supremacists are our biggest threat, and I'm sure ignoring that will also come back to haunt us).

In 1999, the CIA knew al-Qaeda was making plans to attack. By the end of 1999, the United States had arrested an al-Qaeda guy coming in through Canada with 130 pounds of bomb-making materials. He had decided he wanted to blow up Los Angeles International Airport.

In 2000, suicide bombers hit the USS *Cole* in Yemen, and al-Qaeda raised its hand: Me. I did it. Over here. Pay attention. I'm coming for you. By August, President George W. Bush had a memo: al-Qaeda plans to attack. The CIA sent another missive in August to the FBI and the State Department.

Meh. We don't need Arabic speakers.

On a personal level, my career was going well: I made staff sergeant—E6—in four years. The average is about eight years. I was still dead set on proving myself: Twice as hard. Twice as fast. Twice as many hours. Twice as much education.

But I don't think I ever planned to stay in as long as I had at that point. I think that, like a lot of people in their early twenties, I knew I wanted to join the Army, but I hadn't thought past the joining. It's like going to the ocean for the first time: You jump in, but you're not sure you're going to like the water. At first, it's a bit cold. The waves are rough. Everything tastes salty. And then, after a while, you think, *You know what? This is not bad. This is good. I like all these different fish. I like the challenge of staying afloat. I like feeling connected to everything in the ocean with me.*

The first week of September 2001, we went out on a field training exercise. We finished the week with a night jump, and then we rucked back, arriving at about 8:00 a.m. We were tired. We always had to clean our weapons when we got back, so we were all spread out with Q-tips and oil and pipe cleaners, and everything smelled like CLP cleaner and carbon. After we had finished up, I stood in the first sergeant's office and watched on TV as the planes hit the World Trade Center.

I knew I wasn't going anywhere. I thought we'd deploy immediately.

I called my wife to check on her. She hadn't seen the news, so I told her to turn on the TV. We had visited the World Trade Center often and had many photos with the Twin Towers in the background. To us, these two buildings represented power and freedom. Every time we visited New York, we went to the top and felt as if we could reach the sky.

My wife immediately started to cry.

"Please, God, don't let them be Muslim," she said.

It was too late for her prayers to be answered.

As I headed down the hallway from the first sergeant's office, a guy said, "See what your people did?"

"Fuck you," I said. "If we're talking about 'my people,' we're talking about you."

But I couldn't stop thinking about what had happened.

We were so fucking stupid.

I thought about what I had seen at the FBI headquarters: no Muslims, no one listening in on chatter, no one watching the communities that we already knew had bombed the World Trade Center once, as well as attacking American embassies.

So fucking stupid.

When 9/11 happened, the guys in the Arab world—the al-Qaeda guys—they couldn't believe it themselves. They had always thought, *Man, America can figure out what size your underwear is. That's how much they watch you. They know everything.* After 9/11, they knew we were not watching anything. To that point, we had gotten by only by the grace of God—or because people feared us because they gave us a lot more credit than we deserved. They thought, *Oh, I don't want to do that because I'm gonna get caught.*

But it turned out no one was watching.

It's like the insurrection at the Capitol on January 6, 2021. No one was watching. No one was fucking paying attention: *There's no way a bunch of white flag-waving patriots would do that.*

Well, yeah, they did. Every time you become complacent in your house—when you leave the door unlocked—somebody's going to come rob you. You send the vibe: it's an easy job. They marched right up to the Capitol, and they found a way in.

The al-Qaeda guys? They also found a soft target. At the time, you could travel on someone else's air ticket. You know who knew that? Immigrants. Why? Because it was cheaper to buy a two-way ticket than a one-way ticket. I could fly from Alexandria to New York, and then I could give my brother my return ticket, and no one would match the ticket with a passport when he used it to fly home to Alexandria. Nobody knew who was on that plane. The immigrants weren't doing it to be devious. It was just cheaper. But it was easy to get through because, in the United States, the government didn't want to impose on your freedom.

Within hours of the attacks, I called the FBI liaison at the Pentagon.

"I'll do whatever you need me to do," I said. The liaison said they would love to have me come back, but the military had frozen all assignments outside the units.

"The military needs you guys," she said.

"I'm at Fort Bragg in the motor pool fixing vehicles," I said.

"I can't do anything," she said. "The military needs you."

Two days later, my first sergeant started singing a cadence about killing all Muslims. I asked for a moment with him.

"You know that cadence you were singing?" I asked. "You have two Muslims in your unit." He felt bad—he didn't know. And he had no idea I was one of them. I explained that the other guy wished to keep his religious beliefs secret. The first sergeant, whom I respected, apologized.

He called a formation and apologized again. And then he asked me to teach classes about Islam. That's when I became a subject-matter expert overnight. Here's what I told people: What happened on 9/11 had nothing to do with Islam. Al-Qaeda, as well as the Muslim Brotherhood, hijacked the religion and ruined its reputation. They made my neighbors believe that I, a US citizen, should not be there—that I was a terrorist by association.

But I also reminded them of what's great about America: By that time, I had worked closely with a Jewish guy who had given me a job and trusted me with his business. I had worked with Christians and gays and Hindus and even atheists, and I had seen that whether a person was good or bad had nothing to do with religion or sexual orientation or race or nationality.

The al-Qaeda fuckers? Same guys I grew up fighting when I was a kid: their roots were in the Muslim Brotherhood.

I felt that I had a moral obligation to make sure these guys didn't do any more damage—either to my fellow Americans or to the religion that also feels like home to me. I didn't want us to be prejudged because of the actions of a few. And I felt as if fellow Muslim Americans needed a role model: I wanted to stand as the immigrant who came to this country and not only served but succeeded at the highest level.

The special operations recruiter called me.

"You'll have my packet in a week," I said.

AS SOON AS THEY handcuffed us and pulled bags over our heads, I started to hear explosions all around me, as if we'd suddenly found ourselves in a war zone.

From underneath my bag, I began to hear voices all around me: "I quit."

I'd been walking for days, and I smelled sour. Things didn't get better after they removed the bags from our heads. They asked me a bunch of questions, including about a message I'd received from a guy at a bar on the shady side of town.

"I don't know," I said.

Whack!

They hit me so hard I was sure I was going to pass out. And then they hit me again. This was real. This was not a joke. They hit the women, too. One interrogator stood at least six feet, five inches tall and weighed a good 250 pounds. He had a monster beard, like some kind of militant religious terrorist—or a biker—and a bald head.

"Please don't smack me," I said, as I stood eyeball-to-belly button with the biggest guy I had ever seen in my life. "If you smack me again, you're going to kill me. So don't."

He didn't smile.

This was not a war zone.

For days, we had walked. Twenty miles. Thirty miles. Fifty miles. In the desert. In the city. In the woods. We never knew what our days would look like. One MRE to last a day. If we were in the city, eleven dollars to last a day. They dropped us in the worst places: Sand in every direction with no landmarks. The rough parts of town. At one point, I looked so bad, a woman thought I was homeless.

"Hey, I saw you walking around yesterday," she said.

Is this part of it? I thought. *Is this a test?*

I had become paranoid about everything, sure that someone would try to trip me up.

I had been wearing the same clothes for days. I hadn't shaved in a week. She tried to give me money.

"I can't take it," I told her. She insisted. "No, no," I explained. "I'm not homeless."

As it turned out, she had nothing to do with it. She was just kind.

They told us to pack a bag, and when we arrived, we gave it to our evaluators. They then decided what we would wear that first day. Our first day of walking? They gave one of the women a pair of high heels she had packed in her bag. She walked at least twenty miles that day. I am sure she was in pain, but my god, she was fucking tough.

Most of us would not make it through selection. And many of us would not make it through training. By the end of it, I had injured myself enough that I needed cortisone shots. There was no skin on the bottom of my feet.

Was it physical?

Yes.

But mostly, it was a mindfuck.

The process isn't classified. But I'm not going to tell you exactly what was in selection and what was in training, because the integrity of the process is important to me and to the people who continue to serve in the Unit. There will be some crossover between what was in selection and what was in training after I got selected— and even what was in training after I got to the Unit, as well as when I became cadre myself. (Spoiler alert: I made it through training and selection, but I had my moments. Many moments.) But I will tell you how my training affected me personally and how it helped me on my missions.

Not all operatives go through the same things I did, so what I will share is merely my own experience.

Selection doesn't always start the same, but I got my orders. I showed up at the airport, and there was a reception. They had us set our watches. They took our phones.

"Leave your ego at the door," they told us on the first day. Those who didn't failed.

I went in feeling like I was special: Not only had I joined the Army as a non-English-speaking immigrant but I was usually the shortest guy in the group. Well, always. But despite that, I had excelled in training, physical fitness, rank, and education.

But it's like when you go from high school, where you're the best football player at your school, and move on to college, where all the best football players from all the high schools are and you're no longer the best.

That first week at selection, they had all of us put together short presentations about ourselves.

I was not special. Not in this world.

We had a guy who grew up between Brazil and Argentina, a guy whose dad had kidnapped him and taken him to Lebanon and then Libya, a guy who grew up fishing in Alaska, a guy whose family came from Ukraine. One woman was a world-class swimmer. There was a guy who ended up mayor for one day of his hometown in a foreign country after a coup and who then had to flee for his life. You see that and think, *That's fucking amazing. This guy's with me in class.*

Another person was from Nebraska and had never been on a bus in her life.

That's not very amazing, I thought. But she had strong language skills.

One guy, Jacob, had been shot in the face. While the bullet missed his brain, it took out his eye. His party trick? Popping out his glass eye.

Half the students grew up with great hardship and had to work their asses off to get where they were. Everyone was proud of his or her hardship. It was part of who they were. It made them strong and resilient and creative.

It was humbling.

It was humbling for everyone.

Before we arrived, we removed our rank and our tabs—the ones proclaiming that we were airborne and air assault and Ranger and that we could shoot well, which I actually couldn't. We wore uniforms that didn't even have our names on them.

Some folks tried to slide that bit of extra in, but if we showed up with fade marks that showed where we had removed our tabs? It just proved we had no balls (or ovaries—or whatever) because when we wore uniforms without rank or tabs, it meant our confidence had to come from within. It meant we were treated like everybody else—the Puerto Rican woman with the heavy accent or the brown guy who you don't fucking know what he speaks. Racism? Sexism? That comes from having no true confidence— from feeling like you have to be better than *somebody*.

There were people who could not operate without the uniform, without the tabs and the rank and the distinction. They believed people wouldn't respect them as much without the props—maybe even wouldn't listen to them. Without rank and tabs, we had to show our value by using our knowledge, skills, and personality.

That's hard stuff. We had been trained—socialized—to operate on the basis of rank. But in training—and in the Unit—the best-qualified person for a particular job or mission leads it. That could mean a staff sergeant asks a major to take out the trash.

They worked hard to retrain us, to help us think differently.

If we weren't in our tabless uniforms, we could choose what we wanted to wear—what made the most sense to us: military pants plus a T-shirt. Jeans.

Brown shoes.

That taught us flexibility. The world is not just camouflage. They taught us to get out of the institutionalized mindset. In basic training, the military resocializes you—breaks you down and builds you up. Each unit builds on it a bit more: The hierarchy of tabs. The troops who take pride in extreme slacking skills. The pride in unit history. The cool way to blouse boots or iron a uniform that's not supposed to be ironed.

In selection and training, they broke us yet again, but this time, we were not meant to follow the crowd. Did we have guys who drank the Kool-Aid? Absolutely. But Unit operatives tend to have a rebellious spirit underneath the shiny Army shell. The Unit did not want yes-men. It wanted creative thinkers who could figure out how to do the job.

They wanted to see if we had the internal confidence to make that happen.

We tend to say it's mind over matter—you just have to want it and push harder and all of that shit, which is, in part, true. That's great motivation for morning physical training.

But special operations folks are made differently. Or their environments and experiences shape them in a way that's different. Or something.

I'm not just blowing nonsense out of my ass.

In the late 1980s, the Army realized it had wasted a lot of money bombing students out of selection. Think about it: You recruit, you move, you outfit, and you train those people—even if they don't make it past a week. Worse, what if a person makes it most of the way? Then the military's spent thousands on someone who may go back to that job in the cubicle.

The military has looked at everything: How physical training affects candidates' abilities to succeed. How "grit"—yes, there's a grit test—and cortisol and testosterone and height factor in. There have been studies that show operatives are more likely to win in poker matches because they take risks—the right kind of risks. Yes, we can run, but we also have attributes that make us more likely to make ethical decisions and come up with creative ideas under pressure and keep going when things hurt. I don't know if those are things we acquired along the way—because so many of us encountered hardship, perhaps? Or if we had those strong attributes innately—and that's why we succeeded when we encountered hardship.

I think I was lucky. I learned things about myself I hadn't known before. I realized I could do things I didn't think I could do. It challenged me mentally. I gained confidence, and I changed.

The psychologists who came up with the whole thing are geniuses.

But the first two days of selection?

I did everything wrong.

I was coming from the Eighty-Second Airborne Division. I was tactically sound. But on those first ruck marches, I failed completely at navigation. I went back to my bunk bed, and my legs freaking hurt. Forty or fifty miles with a heavy ruck every day will get you. I slung a belt from the bunk above me so I could elevate my legs. I lay there, and my legs were hanging, and I just stared at the bottom of the top bunk.

What am I doing wrong?

No one gave us any feedback—not on how well we did push-ups or how fast we ran the PT tests or how far I was from the coordinate I was supposed to be marching toward—so I didn't even know how badly I was fucking up or if they were going to come tap my shoulder and ditch me. A type A overachiever, and no one was there to tell me if I was overachieving or just sucking ass. And I'd totally been in the category of "Hey, I'm special. Treat me as special." But there I was with my ankles looped into a belt sling, and I was not special. I was just a dude with sore legs who couldn't find his way out of a three-foot-tall maze. I was nervous.

I can't fail, I thought. *If I do, this is going to be a short fucking book.*

I only had one choice.

They invited me, I thought. *So I'm not dumb, and I'm not less than anybody else. They invited me because they believe in me. I like it here. And I'll be damned if I'm going to tell my wife and my team-mates I failed.*

I realized that I just needed to calm myself the fuck down.

I had some blisters, so I took care of them. Then I said a couple of prayers. One of the great things about Islam is that prayers put you in a physical place: You place your forehead on the ground. You face toward Mecca. It's meditative. It's restful. It forces you to breathe.

I remembered moments past: Fasting during Ramadan. Rucking in the snow in Pennsylvania. More rucking at Fort Bragg. I just needed to get my act together. I needed to trust my gut and do what I had trained to do.

No worries, short guy, I said to myself. *You can make it.*

Those few moments allowed me to come to a decision: I would wake up the next morning, and I wouldn't look at anybody else. I wouldn't pay attention to who was around me. I would not consider that anybody else existed. Everybody would just be invisible to me. I pictured victory and thought about how it would feel at the end of selection—what it would be like to be one of America's best.

And then I went to sleep.

The next day, we had to do land nav in a big fucking desert. We walked forever.

I felt as if I got everything right that day.

When I stopped worrying about everyone else, about being watched, I stopped caring about people praising me. Instead, I just did my best. It was the first lesson of selection, and it's a hard lesson for a lot of people. It's natural to want feedback— especially if you're Mr. Run-around-the-Formation-with-the-Guidon-during-Battalion-Runs. Instead, I learned to do what's right because I knew it was right—not because someone was going to give me an award.

I made another decision that helped me succeed. They talked fast. Stupid fast. I spent most of my time trying to catch what they were saying because English is still not my first language. I picked up maybe 20 percent of what they said, so I figured that was the 20 percent I was going to do. I wouldn't worry about the rest. I was no longer nervous or scared; it just felt like a huge challenge.

And of course they meant for it to be a challenge. In both selection and training, they stressed us in every possible way.

It was still only the beginning.

We didn't know how long it would last.

The Special Forces guys—the Green Berets—also go through selection, but it wasn't the same as ours. They knew, going in, exactly what they would encounter during their twenty-one days.

They knew that if they could just suck it up for three weeks, they were golden. They also knew, every day, exactly what they would be doing: Today, I'm going to do this task. I'll need this much food and water. And tonight, I'm going to sleep in this particular spot after a twenty-mile road march. They knew that they would spend much of their time at Camp Mackall in North Carolina.

It may not seem like a big deal, but just that sense of a beginning, a middle, and an end gives you an edge: I only have to do this for another two hours/six miles/three days. Your first question—anybody's first question—will always be, "For how long?" We didn't have that. We didn't even know how long selection would last. Six weeks? Eight weeks? They wanted to know if we were willing to take the risk, as well as if we could muscle through that daily unknown.

Our goals were also different from the Green Berets'. We were not like other elite military organizations. The Unit was more about brains than brawn. That's not a knock on them—they were extremely smart guys. We just had different jobs. For some SOF units, like the SEAL Teams, the more they worked out, the better they were. They needed to be an expert at every weapon and a master of hand-to-hand combat. They excelled at what we call the "hard skills." They might have spent four months out of twelve training on those tasks.

We were selected according to how we could evaluate what's right and what's wrong, how we could evaluate information, and how we could think. Could we storm a house and shoot people? Absolutely. But we rarely needed to, and if we had to, we didn't do it blindly.

But we also had to figure out who the bad guy was—and that

required serious analyzing skills, maybe even overanalyzing skills. It required an ability to role-play. We had to be chameleons, to be able to fit in within every environment.

The main difference between us and other elite military organizations is that we had crazy technical skills. In the Unit, we had the best of both worlds because we knew how to get information but we also knew how to act on it. Find. Fix. Finish. Often, operators from other elite units handled the "finish" part—they were much better at it.

The training for us—the after-selection part—lasted almost a year. They broke it down into three stages: tactical military; nonmilitary strategic; and "let's bring it all together to test you," where you use all of your new skills to perform certain tasks—to figure out puzzles.

They didn't just evaluate whether we passed or failed. They evaluated us mentally and psychologically. How do you deal with others? Are you a dick? Because if you're a dick, you're not going to make it. How do you deal with yourself? How do you do things when you're by yourself? How do you motivate yourself? How smart are you? How scared of things are you; how quickly do you quit; how quickly do you cry? How would you deal with torture and capture?

We were US soldiers being selected and evaluated, both physically and mentally, on whether we could be trained to execute some of the most crucial missions possible.

They chose us because they thought we could fit in, and then they emphasized being gray during selection, training, and thereafter. Were we going through selection for a bigger cause or because it would make us look cool to the women (or men) we wanted to pick up at bars? Hint: men and women at bars should have believed we were infantry or military intelligence or executives on a business trip.

Social media didn't exist, really, when I joined, but when it did, we didn't use it. At all. You wouldn't find us in a Google search while we were in the Unit. If some guy brags to you about being in the Unit, and then you see his Facebook page? He's not telling you the truth.

Being gray could save our lives. If you wanted to be a target, you could walk into a room and make sure everybody in the room knew that you were a military guy—that you were the strongest guy and the fastest guy and the smartest guy.

Who's going to be the first person they shoot?

Some people disappeared—whisked away by the cadre, never to be seen again. We lost more than half of the candidates in my selection. In training, we lost another half of our candidates. It's different for every group.

One guy quit because he couldn't operate his GPS.

"I don't need this shit!" he said, before smashing the device to pieces on the ground. Ranger—I could tell from the shadows on his faded uniform.

Probably he was already a little freaked out. They put a lot of pressure on you. But if this stud soldier quit because of his GPS, how would he deal with the real-world shit?

But this is what selection is for: Can the tough guy keep his cool? Can the quiet guy lead?

We had a Marine in our class—great guy, huge. Proud. He let everybody know just how proud he was to be a Marine.

He didn't make it either.

Some people aren't capable of being gray.

But after that, the Marine continued to serve honorably and became one of the best in his follow-up assignments.

In 2002, while I was in training, I was in Washington, DC, with some Army friends visiting a buddy who had been admitted to Walter Reed Army Medical Center. At the same time, the DC shooter started randomly killing people. As we stood across the street from a gas station, we heard a gunshot. A man had been shot. The three of us ran across the street and tried to save him. But the man was too far gone to revive. He may have already been dead when we started.

We got awards for that, but we were like, "Hey, please don't make a fuss."

Because we wanted to be gray. We asked that there be no publicity and that they not use our names.

When I was an instructor, a good friend of mine was a psychological evaluator. He could predict who would make it—just spot on: "Bob's not going to make it. Bob's gonna quit." They tried to eliminate people before the government spent a lot of time training them. We heard that it cost more than $1 million to train each operative. (I never had that figure confirmed, but it seems about right.) The Unit's budget is classified, but a select few members of Congress are aware of it.

When I was a part of the cadre, we made a bet one time about who would quit first. We put up a board.

There was a big guy, Ranger qualified, physically fit, in that class. My friend put him up on the board for the first one to quit.

"Man, naw," I said.

The candidates went out on their first march, and, of course, it was a long one—a very, very fucking long one. The cadre were set up at different points along the route, and the candidates were meant to report something to us, and then we would give them their next instructions.

I could see the Ranger coming at me.

He was struggling.

Dude who was Ranger qualified was struggling.

He dangled his head and dragged his feet.

Nobody quits in the first part. This guy still had a long way to go.

But I could see it in his eyes.

He got closer.

Don't quit, I thought. *Don't fucking quit.*

As he got to me, he dropped his rucksack.

"I fucking quit," he said.

We got him off the course so the others couldn't see him.

A lot of people have fake motivation—"I can't let somebody see me in pain, or struggling, or hurting." I may have been one of those guys. The guy who quit? He didn't care.

I radioed the psych.

"Jay," I said, "you won. Your guy quit."

I saw people quit three hours before the end of selection—they never learned how close they had been.

But people made things hard on themselves, too. People overengineered things. When I was selection cadre, we gave the students tasks that probably seemed dumb to them: every time you sit down, sit this way and put your equipment in this position. We wanted to make sure they could pay attention to detail. But with some guys, we had to say it over and over and over again. Maybe they were tired? Maybe they were so happy to sit down that they forgot? It says a lot about how candidates handle everything. How they shine their boots tells me how they're going to do when somebody tells them to tuck in their bootlaces in airborne school. What we told them to do had meaning, even if they didn't know it. They had to trust us.

And some people just love fucking shortcuts. Someone is watching the candidates at pretty much every moment—to evaluate, to keep them safe—but some people just can't help themselves. They've worked so hard just to get into the program, but if given the opportunity for an easy out, they'll take it. Maybe they justify it to themselves as they're doing it? "Maybe they'll think I'm worthy because I was handed an opportunity and I took it?"

Nope.

We thought they were lazy. We thought they couldn't be trusted. We thought they couldn't follow directions.

Candidates were supposed to walk everywhere. The cadre told them that. But we saw people jump on a bus. *Okay*, we thought, *you have no integrity*. That could cost somebody's life.

We didn't want those people. One or two fell through the cracks, but it was rare. Before selection even began, the candidates went through psych evaluations—and those guys were good. They just knew. And all of the cadre members were operatives, and they knew whom they wanted on a mission with them and whom they definitely did not want on a mission with them.

Some people—strong, talented people with Special Forces tabs and long careers—cried when we told them they didn't make it. Those were the people who tried hard but just weren't a good fit for the Unit.

Selection wasn't easy. It's not easy for anybody. They make sure you physically can't take it anymore, and then they make sure you can't take it mentally anymore, either.

In some parts of the course, we carried really, really heavy stuff—and it was never convenient. There would be no handle to carry your load. It would be like carrying a bowling ball rather than a kettlebell: they made it as awkward as possible.

No matter how big or small we were, and no matter whether we were male or female, we performed the same tasks. Even though I'm pretty sure I was the smallest guy in the Army, I carried the same weight as everyone else. When we jumped out of airplanes, they gave me the heaviest rucksack because I was the lightest guy—and then I would have to ruck twenty kilometers with the radio and extra batteries.

Every one of my steps counted for half of a tall guy's step, so I ran to keep up.

Being smaller didn't have many advantages.

We went through a couple of obstacle courses, but not like normal ones. We might encounter a ladder that looked as if it were built for giants or a well we had to climb out of, or they might make us go through part with our hands behind our heads. And yeah, monkey bars, but we had already hit muscle failure by the time we got to them.

We found out during selection if we had any crazy phobias: we jumped from heights; we spent time in the water; we slept in the woods by ourselves.

"If you see a bear, don't try to fight it," they told us, and then they sent us out into the woods for days and days (and nights) for a land-nav course.

In the middle of fucking nowhere in West By-God Virginia, we did a lot of land nav without GPS. They gave us maps and told us where to go, and then we found our spots and camped out. If you grew up in the country, this may seem like no big deal. But I didn't grow up near anything that looked like a forest.

I definitely never saw a bear in Egypt.

Bears are faster than you think. They can run after you. And it was dark. And there were all sorts of noises when we were in the woods by ourselves worrying about what exactly we were supposed to do if we saw a bear if we were not supposed to fight it and we were not supposed to run.

"Hey, bear. Would you like a spot of tea?"

Right. I would find a cozy place for my sleeping bag, and I would eat an eighth of the one MRE they gave me, and then it was dark and . . .

Did you hear something?

I did. I could hear people walking nearby—probably other trainees, even though we weren't supposed to crisscross one another.

When I was an instructor, people got so lost during that portion of the training that they weren't even on base anymore. But that didn't automatically mean they failed. It did mean they needed improvement, but the organization was good at looking at the whole picture. They might have sucked at land nav, but they might have been excellent in a language or planning or problem-solving. And did they fail because they got so scared? Did they panic and find a hole and stay in the hole for three days? Did they give up? Did they figure out a solution when their socks got wet because it never stopped fucking raining? Did they try hard and keep going even though they were beyond lost?

There were times when I thought, *Am I lost? Am I that lost?*

And then I'd hear a car.

Probably I'm going to be okay.

Just before we did that portion of the training, I had injured my foot falling on black ice during a ruck march, so they gave me some steroid shots. With my rucksack, my foot was even more painful, but I learned to numb the pain. I was so focused—it never occurred to me to quit. I just focused on succeeding, and then I didn't feel anything but that need.

Oddly enough, that's normal for guys like me. The people who make it through? They never thought about quitting. I don't think it's intentional. I think our determination and our motivation took over and we didn't even feel anything else. The guys who think, *Should I quit now? Or should I see if I can make it through this training?* have already quit.

Sometimes, we stayed in shady areas where hotels were typically rented by the hour, not by the night. I was afraid to shower in the bathrooms. There could be a drug dealer in the room on one side of me and a prostitute on the other side. I heard odd noises and yelling, and I had a woman knock on my door one night because she assumed I could sell her drugs.

There were no alarm clocks, no phones, no watches. At the end of the day, they'd drop us off at a different hotel in a different place and say, "Be ready at five thirty." Somehow, every morning, I woke up and was ready on time—no matter what time they had said. I would just sit and wait until the guy came and told me what to do next.

And that's what they wanted to teach us: we've got an internal clock, and we're capable, and we just need to trust it.

They wanted us to understand the value of time—how much we could accomplish in one minute. If formation was at 9:00 a.m., that's when everyone magically appeared. So, if it was 8:58 and you realized you needed to use the bathroom, you learned you actually had time to do that. (Plus handwashing.) We began to understand what we could do in short periods of time.

One morning, I was told to meet a guy at a bar at 10:00 a.m. That's all I knew. I started the day at 6:00 a.m., so I had already been walking for four hours. I got there early—at about 9:30 a.m.—so I found a spot on the street to wait. It had to be far enough away that no one could see me because they told us to be exact about our timing. I sat, exhausted, on a street corner until it was time.

Then I went to the bar. I ordered a Coke because I had only four dollars. A guy came in and sat next to me. He began to speak.

I could not understand him.

I couldn't tell if he had an accent or if he was faking an accent. I didn't know if it was part of the show: Was I not supposed to understand what he was saying? But I could see that he was angry. I have an accent, too, so I get how frustrating it can be. I asked him again. He said it one more time, but I just couldn't get it.

And then the fucker got up and left—and didn't pay for his drink. I didn't have enough to leave a tip, and I felt bad about it.

It took a lot of work to keep my head straight, to keep reality separate from my imagination—or my paranoia.

We learned to look for the sun. We learned to look for landmarks far off in the distance. Hot during the day, cold at night. In the morning, the water in my canteen would be frozen. One MRE a day.

It sucked.

They gave us tasks to do as individuals and as groups, but they didn't necessarily have a solution—or the solution was difficult to find. So they would say, "There's a helicopter crash in Libya, and five guys are about to die there. You need to find them, and you need to move them from point A to point B." They would give us some tools, or they might tell us we couldn't use anything except what we found at the crash site. At the crash site, we might find a rope, a chair, a couple of belts, and a tree log. Then we needed to make a meal out of that shitty soup sandwich.

At the site, the psychologists watched and evaluated us. Everything was subjective, so we didn't know how well or poorly we did. I might think we found the best solution, but the psych might think it was the worst solution, or it took us too long, or one of us took over and didn't let other people voice their solutions. They watched to see how we solved problems together, but we never learned how we did.

Some people would fight for power. Some people were just natural. They didn't want the loudest guy in the room—the one who pushed everyone else aside and told people what to do. There was no rank; there was no race; there was no gender.

And then they made us walk some more.

We did a lot of combative training—hand-to-hand fighting. Even in training, they wanted us to be forceful so we would get it right, but we were still not meant to hurt our partners. As we trained one day, the former mayor who had to flee his country was learning how to do a wrist hold to put someone in a painful position. He practiced with another trainee.

We all heard the snap.

He broke her hand. He didn't know how strong he was.

She was in a cast for a couple of months, but she still made it.

During the course, we learned from people who were experts in their fields. They explained how they would react to a situation: how they drive their cars, how they disappear into a crowd, how they follow someone.

The cadre also did things that didn't seem to make any sense: Here. Read this book. Then somebody might ask me about what I had read—or they might not. Or they might ask me to draw a map or a picture of something I'd seen. I did a lot of things without understanding why I did them and without ever finding out why I did them. All of that allowed them to evaluate how I reacted to the unknown.

They didn't mess around. When we did defensive-driving training, it wasn't a check in a box so your commander could say it had been done. We trained until we were exhausted—until long after we were ready to be done. It had to be automatic.

For the counterinterrogation training, they brought in professional interrogators.

Smack!

It's different for everyone, but we were on the West Coast, and the weather was gorgeous, and we were relaxed because we had gone through some rough training, and we all knew one another pretty well at that point. It was, of course, a great group.

One night, we stayed, as a group, at a hotel. All of a sudden, a bunch of guys stormed our room and arrested us.

Okay. What the fuck?

An old lady in the next room saw all of it, and it freaked her out pretty hard. We're probably lucky we didn't end up a meme for police brutality.

They weren't pretending. They smacked the fuck out of me.

We had a guy, I'll call him Mike, with us who was extraordinarily smart, to the point that he overengineered everything and was incapable of working with other people because he was smarter than everybody else. Hilarious, though, and I liked him. He and I were in the same room for one interrogation—picture a gym or an old-school barracks with an open shower area. I swear I could smell sweaty socks, bleach, and Speed Stick.

The interrogator asked me a question.

"I don't know," I said.

Smack!

They told us not to talk too much.

The interrogator asked Mike a question.

Mike told the interrogator this long-ass story.

"Mike," the interrogator said, "you talk too much."

But he couldn't stop. And every time he talked more, the interrogator smacked him again. Smacked him hard. Extremely hard.

Whoa, I thought. *This is real.*

C'mon, man. Shut up. Just shut the fuck up.

Smack!

They hit him so hard he almost passed out, but he just couldn't stop. It was part of his makeup, and it had probably worked well for him at every other point of his life—because he was so fucking smart. But the interrogators were doing him a kindness by trying to teach him—and he couldn't help himself.

You know that point in the movie where the bad guy interrogates the good guy, and the bad guy asks a question, and the good guy responds with some smart-ass, fabulous, funny line? And then the bad guy beats the fuck out of the good guy—or pulls out his fingernails or cuts off his pinkie? And you think, *Wow. That was a good line, but boy, was that dumb.*

You're right.

That's dumb.

We learned to use some common sense: If the answer is yes or no, answer yes or no. Don't try to be clever. Don't keep talking. Don't think that the more you say, the better your lie.

You've seen that movie, too. It never works out.

Don't punch him back. That should be obvious, right?

"What's your name?" the interrogator asked one of my teammates.

And he told him. He told him his real name.

The interrogator came to me ████████████████████████
██

"Is Mike his real name?"

For fuck's sake.

"Dude," I said, "you smacked him so hard that he fucking forgot his name. That's not my problem. That's your problem."

"He just told us his name is Mike," he said.

"I know; his name is George," I said. "Not Mike. I don't know who the fuck Mike is."

They'd roughed me up. I hadn't eaten. My brain struggled to find fuel, and I still didn't know what I was supposed to tell them and what I was not supposed to tell them. They asked me what the guy at the bar told me.

"I don't know," I said.

"He told you twice," they said.

"Honestly, I don't have any idea what he said because of his accent."

"What language did you think he spoke?"

"Spanish," I said.

"Didn't you think it might be important enough to ask him to say it in Spanish?" they said.

"I don't speak Spanish."

"I thought you were a fucking Mexican."

"I'm a fucking Egyptian."

Whack!

But they wanted us to be wily, too—to make the best of what we had.

Or what we didn't have, in Jacob's case.

Whack! An interrogator hit Jacob upside the head.

He hit him so hard his glass eyeball popped right out of its socket.

"Holy shit!" the interrogator yelled.

"Oh my god!" I screamed. "What did you do?"

Oscar-worthy, I'm telling you. I opened my own eyes wide.

"Now he's blind!" I yelled.

It was exactly what I had learned to do in my training. Everyone looked horrified, pure panic. It was amazing. It took everything I had not to laugh.

Somehow, we both made it through training.

They wanted to get our attention, to let us know what we might be in for. The job was no joke. Doing it right might make a difference not only for ourselves and our coworkers but for our nation's security.

Ultimately, the decisions we made could require great personal sacrifice.

As a soldier, I had also needed to be prepared for sacrifice. But generally speaking, if the bad guys got me, a team of muscled humans would come after them: no soldier left behind.

After training, there would be instances where I would be invisible. I would be alone. And I would be told that if the mission failed, I was on my own.

Aden Ayro.

Jackpot.

The lessons we learned during interrogation were important.

And Danny Pearl changed everything. While reporting for the *Wall Street Journal* in February 2002—while I was in training—he was tricked into a meeting, taken hostage, and then beheaded by al-Qaeda terrorists in Pakistan. They posted video of it. It was a huge wake-up call for everyone. We changed our training methodology after that.

A car thief taught me how to get out of handcuffs in the back of a car. And he taught me how to unlock the trunk from the inside. But my instructors also taught me that if somebody got me into the trunk of a car, I was fucked. By the time you get the trunk open, they've already driven you someplace you don't want to be.

Escape. Get your ass out of there quickly. If you pull out a gun, it's not to scare somebody. It's to kill somebody. It's not time to injure him so he can't chase you: if you aim at his foot, you're going to miss it. Shoot to kill. If you don't want to have to kill somebody, the best way to get out of a situation is to not get into the situation.

Fight your way out.

Because otherwise, they're going to cut off your head—
especially if you're a Muslim guy serving in the US military. They
would have enjoyed it.

We saved a few people—including civilians—who were in
those situations in Iraq. They were lucky. And we were lucky that,
in less than twenty-four hours, we were able to get them out.

That guy broke my heart. Danny Pearl.

During the interrogation training, we knew we could answer
questions when "the ambassador" showed up.

I refused to talk, and I refused to talk, and I refused to talk, and
then they brought in the ambassador.

"Okay, I need you to tell them what you remember from the
last few days," he said. "We're testing your memory."

I sat down with a pen and paper and just wrote down everything. Everything. I have a great memory. I wrote every single
detail: Who I saw. What I had for breakfast. Where I walked. How
I completed my tasks.

They stopped me after about an hour and a half.

I met the interrogator again about two years later—after I was
in the Unit.

"Nobody could understand the guy with the accent," he told
me. "We knew he couldn't speak English very well."

And my interrogator? The big guy with the beard? He was a
priest—the nicest guy. He said it took everything he had not to
bust out laughing when I told him not to smack me.

Just his plain hugeness was enough to make him a good interrogator. They make it as real as possible.

We trained and trained and trained. We didn't pass until they
knew we could really figure it out.

All through it, they kept us walking. I had no skin left on the bottom of my feet. I had landed sideways fast roping out of a Blackhawk and twisted my ankle the wrong way. My knee still ached from slipping on the black ice—the doctor had told me not to run on it for six months. And I was exhausted. I hadn't been able to eat enough to keep any weight on my body, and I could feel it breaking down.

I was so fucking thirsty.

Should I quit?

I couldn't even move. Couldn't move my feet.

A member of the cadre in a car rolled up next to me.

Shit.

I knew I was done. I knew he had come to tell me I had failed. I got in the car.

But he didn't say anything.

Shit. He's taking me somewhere else to make me walk some more. Should I tell him I can't walk anymore?

He handed me a bag.

"Eat this," he said. "We're going home."

It was the best burger I've ever eaten.

I HAD COMPLETED MY hard-core, secret-squirrel, badass Unit training, and it was time for me to launch into the world. Oakleys on, sleeves rolled up, USA baseball cap in place.

Boom! Interrogator.

You might recall that I had requested to be an interrogator long before the military spent a million bucks to build me into a sparkly new fighting machine.

Yeah. The government was exactly that desperate for people who spoke Arabic, Pashtu, Dari, and Farsi.

I had deployed almost immediately upon arriving at the Unit. First, I hit a Gulf country to start looking at how people were moving through the world to become terrorists.

That was before the Iraq invasion in March 2003.

Where I ended up pretty much immediately after the initial push. I figured I'd get there, catch my breath, maybe deal with the jet lag. Unpack.

Instead, on my first night in Iraq, after my team chief, Robbie, and I loaded our shit in a deuce and a half, we sat on top of our shit in the back of the deuce and a half. And after we then were dropped, with our shit, at a palace, where we unloaded our shit into a room that we immediately had to move out of, the sergeant major came in.

"Hey, we're going out, and we're going to need you guys," he said.

We didn't even have our equipment ready.

"Right," Robbie said. "We'll figure it out." That's pretty much how he moved through life—not all supermotivated so much as zen—the guys called him "Snow Monkey" because he had a massive beard and liked to sit low on his haunches like a Buddhist orangutan. He helped me with my helmet, night-vision goggles, radio, body armor that weighed a third as much as I did, and all my other shit. I was the FNG all over again. Robbie and I went out, and I rode in a vehicle with this old guy. I talked to him as if he were just an old-ass sergeant major—that's what he looked like. Smokin' and jokin' and wondering at how squared away his gear was.

We took a break between hits.

"Hey, man," Robbie said. "You might want to talk to the old guy with a little bit more respect."

"I got this, man," I said. "We're just talking."

"Yeah, but he's a general."

"He's a what?" I said. "How the fuck am I supposed to know he's a general?"

McChrystal.

We finished out the mission with a total of about six hits—picking up bad guys—and we went back, and we had to do an after-action review. McChrystal took off his flak vest. I saw one or two stars on his collar. Brilliant. This would be Stanley McChrystal, who, by the end of 2003, would serve as the SOF Task Force commander. We loved him because he said, out loud, what he thought—to his troops, to his leaders, to the media, and even to the president. He had been to the Persian Gulf before, during Desert Storm, and he had been through every bit of the tough training. He was worthy of more respect than I had given him. On the other hand, he had seemed to enjoy the banter. McChrystal went up front and started to talk.

I can't believe I was sitting next to that motherfucker, I thought, *talking to him like he was some gnarly old sergeant.*

But that's the thing with McChrystal: even as a task force commander, he did everything with us. We would have followed him anywhere.

We all (except for General McChrystal) lived together in this beautiful, scenic spot in a palace in the Green Zone. Seabees (Navy guys who can build anything) came and built bunk beds for us, and there were five of us in one room. We were surrounded by beautiful mosaics, gilded columns, and even a swimming pool—and the guys were just bored. Leadership thought we were each some kind of magician and could make something out of nothing, but we simply didn't have the equipment appropriate for such a mission.

But we had been trained, more than anything else, for adaptability. And we needed interrogators.

The towers had been hit in 2001. A thinking person might suppose that the military brought in as many Arabic speakers as it could. That person would be incorrect. Things didn't look any different for the military, as far as translators, two years after the 9/11 terrorist attacks than they had at the FBI when I helped translate the al-Qaeda manual before the attacks.

In 2002, the Army reported, it could only find forty-two of the eighty-four Arabic linguists it needed to hire. The Center for Army Lessons Learned at Fort Leavenworth, Kansas, found that "the lack of competent interpreters throughout the theater impeded operations."[16]

But rather than holding on to people with those skills, the military, directed by Congress, worked to get rid of them.

In fact, from 1994 to 2003—just as things were starting to heat up—the military booted 322 people who spoke key foreign languages, including Arabic, Farsi, and Korean, out of the military for being gay, under the "don't ask, don't tell" policy.

But things didn't get better after the government realized we desperately needed those translators—and as many boots on the ground as we could get. Talent. People who think outside the box simply because they've had to. By 2006, more than 11,000 gay and lesbian service members had been dismissed under the policy—including 726 in 2005. Of those, 300 had critical language skills, including fifty-five who spoke Arabic, according to the Government Accountability Office.

Brilliant.

---

16 Ann Scott Tyson, "Uzbek or Dari? Military Learns New Tongues," *Christian Science Monitor*, January 2, 2004, https://www.csmonitor.com/2004/0102/p03s01-usmi.html.

Because the military is not a social experiment, right?

It cost millions of dollars—and so much wasted time—to re-place them.

It wasn't just the military: a study from the University of Mary-land said the FBI, the CIA, and many other government agencies all faced a "critical shortage" of Arabic linguists,[17] as I had seen at FBI headquarters.

At the unit level, as expected, we also had a huge shortage of interrogators who spoke Arabic. But they gave us a guy—Frankie—who was from a National Guard unit in California. He spoke Chinese.

Which was helpful.

In any case, they needed my Arabic skills.

We worked in what looked like an old jail with cells inside the airport complex. It was a decent place. The detainees weren't in bad conditions, but they weren't treated like royalty, either. At first, I just observed the interrogations to see what information the interrogators were getting. We had civilian linguists—native speakers—from Dearborn, Michigan, as well as some other places in the States. But as I watched, I saw a huge gap between the guy doing the interrogation and the guy doing the translation.

Our translators were contractors. The Army would go to a big defense contractor and say, "I need fifty linguists." And the companies would come up with fifty breathing humans quickly so they could make money off the government. If you could say "good morning" in Arabic, hired! We ended up with Farsi lin-

17 NPR, "Turning 'Unfriendly Fire' on U.S. Military's Gay Ban," *Fresh Air*, June 16, 2009, https://www.npr.org/templates/story/story.php?storyId=105441652.

guists who said they spoke Arabic. Had we been in Iran or Afghanistan, that would have been perfect. But we were in Iraq, and Farsi wasn't going to do anybody a damn bit of good.

In a couple of situations, the military guys caught the bad interpreters right away.

We called them "terps"—short for "interpreters." It's not a term everyone recalls fondly, but it's the reality. In any case, as I listened, I realized they weren't translating accurately, or they put their own salt and pepper on it. If we were talking with an Iraqi Sunni and the interpreter was Shia, he would change some things or leave things out. More than once, I saw the civilian interpreter yell at the detainee. That's a no-go.

We wanted to know how foreign fighters were getting into Iraq.

To that end, I was in and out of Iraq in 2003, including visits to another Gulf state where they had some al-Qaeda training camps. Government, so acronyms for everything: AQAP—al-Qaeda Arabian Peninsula. AQEA—al-Qaeda East Africa. AQM—al-Qaeda Morocco, which included Morocco, Tunisia, and Algeria. And so on. They were like al-Qaeda franchises. This was when we realized how huge the network was.

And that's when General Stanley McChrystal, as task force commander, started saying, "It takes a network to defeat a network."

That was us. We were a part of that network. We built it from scratch with operators of every color, shape, and gender. We could not operate like a regular Army unit against an entity that did not play by our rules, McChrystal said. Obviously, we didn't play by their rules entirely, but McChrystal broke all kinds of barriers.

He trusted us to know what we needed. So, as a staff sergeant in 2003—basically at a section-sergeant level—if I said I needed $500,000 worth of equipment because I was going to do something important with it, there was no red tape. McChrystal knew we needed to be agile to defeat al-Qaeda.

We shared everything, which was new. People tend to be greedy about information—except gossip. So if there was an al-Qaeda guy in Mali getting ready to move through Egypt to Syria and then to Iraq, our guy in Africa made sure everybody down the chain knew.

I hope it's still the same. I doubt it's still the same. McChrystal was incredible. He broke the barriers between government agencies, so JSOC was on a task force with many other government agencies. Hell, one time in Iraq, we had a couple of New York police officers on the task force for crowd training or something. McChrystal did not stand for people who did not play well with others. He was a true soldier-diplomat.

He used to conduct round-robins where everyone would call in. But he didn't just talk about the mission. He'd say, "I've been reading this book about the history of Iraq."

And I'd think, *When in the fuck does this guy have time to read?*

He also asked each of us to talk about what we thought and why we thought it.

He led us, but he taught us, too.

He stayed in Iraq and Afghanistan for a long time. I don't know how the guy maintained his marriage. But his wife, Annie, seemed pretty amazing, too.

As I was learning the ropes, I was also learning the team. While they were different from anything I had experienced before, some things never change: we fucked with one another constantly. It was a way to learn camaraderie and relieve stress, but it also allowed us to get to know one another. I had felt welcomed pretty much instantly—especially after Robbie took me aside, told me I was good, and asked me to let him know if I needed anything. All of the guys were like that—hooking me up with gear and advice and stories. I never encountered any racism from my immediate group. They were all too confident in their own abilities and too open-minded about the world for any of that shit.

In some cases, they were maybe a little too confident.

Robbie was small—just three inches taller than I am—which meant that people who didn't know him liked to mess with him. The day before Thanksgiving one year, we all played football and relaxed at an embassy in the Middle East. Robbie showed up, and he was wearing his Doc Martens—they added some height. This civilian agency guy kept giving him shit for being short—like aggressively, chip-on-his-shoulder, what-the-hell? giving him shit. Big, tall dude. Maybe six feet, two inches. Robbie was five feet, four inches.

At first, Robbie just laughed it off. Whatever, dude.

But the guy kept going at it—so much that everyone was like, "Hey, asshole."

But we all knew he was the number two guy at the embassy. There were embassy Marines and some security guys at this gathering. We decided to let it roll off; there's always an asshole.

Dude made another short joke.

Out of nowhere, Robbie rushed the guy, grabbed him around the knees, lifted him as high in the air as he could, twisted him around, and then just slammed him into the ground.

The first thing that hit was the guy's back, and everyone heard it. Dead silence.

Robbie was a Division I wrestler. He knew exactly how to shock the hell out of that guy without hurting him.

The next day? Thanksgiving. About twenty-four hours later, the guy still had the same look of disbelief on his face. Robbie smiled at him.

This was my team leader. He was also aggressively chill. His attitude was always, "We'll get it sorted"—just as he had been when we went out with McChrystal on our first night in-country. The other members of the team were just as great, just as smart and creative and quick as you would expect. I always felt like the dumbest guy in the room because the skill set and experience and knowledge were extreme.

I felt as if I had found my people.

Because of McChrystal's mission to create a network, when the assaulters went out on a hit, one of our guys was usually there too, gathering information, guiding.

So during the day, I went out on hits with the guys, and then at night, I would continue the interrogations we had begun when we had grabbed the detainees. That was great because I had seen what their houses looked like and met their families—I already had a bit of a personal reference, but they didn't know it was me. We were all geared up, and I didn't speak Arabic when we went out.

Because I wasn't a trained interrogator, I went about it differently: I thought about the human side. It's possible that part of that came from interrogating people who look like me—I saw them as human—but part of that was just how I do things. I definitely was not calling everybody Hajji (I've made the trip to

Mecca myself) or Achmed (I mean, unless the guy's name was Achmed). And I definitely had a better cultural understanding of what might work and what definitely would not work.

Bill Clinton, when he talked about Rwanda, probably said it best when he said that dehumanizing a group makes it a lot easier to kill them. Armies have done this for generations—ours and theirs—and it makes it a hell of a lot harder to recover. I remember that George W. Bush kept comparing Iraq to Germany after World War II—as if Germany had been our enemy but we helped them rebuild after the war and we all lived happily ever after.

But the Germans didn't have centuries of history with the Allies trying to destroy them. The Germans looked like the Allies. The majority of Germans were Christians, like the majority of Allies.

The Germans didn't see the Allies as the Crusaders coming back for another round. Germany also did not have tribal warfare—a rush to see who would get to be the next strongman.

You could even look at our own country after World War II—at what Japanese American citizens faced. Or Arab Americans after 9/11. If we teach young Americans to dehumanize groups, it changes the face of "peacekeeping" missions, as well as potentially teaching people a lifetime of hate. Clinton talked about that in Iraq—about how some US troops treated dogs better than they treated the people. You still hear some service members and veterans talking about "nuking the Middle East into glass."

Long after Iraq became a peacekeeping mission, we couldn't get good information or create steady partnerships or build strong trust. It's not hard to figure out why. We did have guys who went out and painted schools and installed generators and helped train medical personnel, but it wasn't enough to convince the Iraqis that we were good people. Both sides—us with our *RoboCop* gear and them with their "man dresses"—had been dehumanized. How do you bridge that gap?

We had our own detention center at ████████████████—and we were authorized to keep people for twenty-one days. After that, we either released them or sent them to the Army. A regular Army unit was in charge of the detention center. They had been sent to Iraq to handle any weapons of mass destruction the military found, because they were an NBC unit: nuclear, biological, and chemical weapons. We all know how that turned out: no WMD. The unit had nothing better to do, so they, with no training as military police, guarded prisoners. I'm not saying the guys we were with did a bad job, just that they weren't trained to do the job. They basically listened to anyone who told them what to do.

The interrogators themselves weren't making much progress. I sat in on some of the interrogations to translate, and they asked questions like, "Hey, which mosque in Syria? Where are they radicalizing you and telling you to go fight in Iraq?"

"That's a stupid question," I told the interrogator. "I'm not translating that for you."

"Well, why is that a stupid question?"

"Because every mosque in Syria does that," I said. "There is no specific mosque."

He asked him anyway. And the guy said, "Every mosque does that."

"Man, just let me do this," I said.

So that's how I ended up doing more interrogations and getting more information. The interrogator would come with me and write the report.

It's not that the interrogator wasn't smart. He just didn't have the cultural background to understand why his questions wouldn't bring good information.

I started building some rapport with the detainees. I sat on the floor with them. I gave them food. And then I just talked with them. Some of them didn't even know where they were—they had been picked up in Mosul up north and then flown to Baghdad. During the flight, they wore bags over their heads. Then I showed up and start talking with them in Egyptian Arabic.

They thought they were in Egypt.

Of course, we used the old interrogation techniques: good cop, bad cop. The good guy is nice to them for a bit, and then the bad cop scares them for a bit.

If a guy cooperated, we'd reduce his deprivation in exchange for information and cooperation.

But it was not torture. Beatings were not authorized, and I never witnessed them.

We had been put in the same conditions in our training. It was uncomfortable. It sucked. The parts of our training that were torture? The beatings? I learned that the more they hurt me, the more I didn't want to talk. I got so angry at the interrogator that I didn't want to give him anything. It's not an effective method. But if you are patient and you have time, people will talk. We learned that there is often a set amount of time for interrogations—before they switch you out for the next guy—so usually, you just have to wait it out. The al-Qaeda guys probably know that, too.

I had an advantage because I need so little sleep. I could sit with a guy for hours. I would eat with him, and I would sit with him while he smoked. (I hate the smell of smoke.) I'd make the guy laugh. I would ensure that he knew I had nothing better in the world to do than to sit with him. After a while, they would get tired.

For me, it felt intuitive. I would think about what it had been like growing up in Alexandria. If a guy grew up in a similar city, I would ask about his childhood. Did you have to wear a uniform? Did you walk to school with your brothers? Did you share a bedroom with your brother? Then I could connect things back to his family, as well as to the kind of financial situation he came from. What was his motivation? Did he want bragging rights, or did he believe it was a crusade?

From a cultural standpoint, Eastern culture is a culture of shame. I used that. I didn't say, "Killing people is bad." That didn't work. He'd be like, "I don't fucking care." But "What would your mom think?" worked. You shame him.

I'm not sure our interrogators are trained to think about those things—we can't have a one-size-fits-all program. If you're interrogating a Muslim person from Chechnya, it's not the same as interrogating a Muslim person from Saudi Arabia.

One of the detainees has always stuck with me. He was from Morocco and young, maybe eighteen. His family sent him to Syria to go to school, but during his summer vacation, he decided to go to Iraq to fight because he bought into the hype. This was a college kid.

He had to be the unluckiest guy on the planet. He had just gotten to the farm—sort of the intake/training center for foreign fighters in Iraq—about two hours before we went there and detained everybody. They were making IEDs and training people how to blow things up. Their number one target? Shia Muslims.

We had intercepted a letter from Abu Musab al-Zarqawi, which was later published on the internet, telling people he wanted them to kill nonbelievers—the Shia. This wasn't a surprise. Zarqawi had been involved in the assassination of US diplomat Laurence Foley in Jordan in 2000 and had spent some time in prison. He'd grown up a poor, uneducated street thug in Jordan, then hooked up with bin Laden in Afghanistan. Even bin Laden thought he was extreme. In Afghanistan, he ran a terrorist training camp—but he worked things in Iraq, too, including suicide bombings to kill US soldiers and beheadings to generally terrify everybody, and he started, or at least added fuel to, the civil war between the Shia and Sunni in Iraq. He joined al-Qaeda in 2004.

But our guys didn't understand the cultural makeup of the region, either—who supported whom. I remember that a SEAL Team guy talked about how Bahrain was an ally, and he had no understanding that while Bahrain's constitutional monarchy may have been an ally, the majority-Shia people they ruled might not be so eager about the Americans.

Quick primer: Saddam Hussein was Sunni, as were his generals. The majority of Iraqis are Shia.

Iran? Shia.

Saudi Arabia? Sunni.

Egypt? Sunni.

Most of the Islamic world is Sunni. But in Iraq, Bahrain, and Iran, Shia are the majority. Both groups—Sunni and Shia—believe the words of the Quran, but they see differences in the

Hadith, which is basically the history of everything Muhammad said or did and is used to guide people's behavior.

The two groups pray differently; the Shia practice temporary marriages, and the Sunni do not; Sunni and Shia women wear hijab—the veil—differently; and they name their children differently, which makes it fairly easy to know if a person is Sunni or Shia.

The difference between Sunni and Shia? The Sunnis believe Abu Bakr, whose daughter Aisha was married to the Prophet Muhammad, should have succeeded the Prophet when he died.

The Shia believe Muhammad's successor was meant to be Ali, the cousin of the Prophet. Ali married Fatimah, who was Muhammad's favorite daughter.

This all happened in the seventh century.

In Iraq, the minority ruled the majority, with the Sunni occupying all the leadership roles under Saddam.

Anyway, we wanted to know from the Moroccan kid how the foreign fighters were getting to Iraq. For this kid, it was like summer camp. I almost felt bad for him. He was this weak, introverted kid who had been bullied his whole life and probably came to Iraq to prove he was a man. I wanted to know how he got his money. His brother washed dishes in Spain and gave him the money. His father had died.

I knew the Moroccan culture, and I knew that his family sent him to Syria with good intentions: to get an education.

"Your two younger sisters look at you as a role model," I said. "And what would your mother think if she knew you came here using the money your brother earned working hard washing dishes?"

It didn't take fifteen minutes before he started to cry. He cried forever. He responded to shame, but he also responded to someone speaking kindly to him in Arabic. He was still terrified—he thought we were going to torture him. This was after Abu Ghraib.

That kid gave me everything.

We gave him a map, and he pointed out exactly which travel agency in Syria helped him, where he got recruited, how he crossed the border, how he got to the farm.

But I also talked to him, because I didn't want to lose the chance to help this kid grow up to be something besides a terrorist. I asked him what he wanted out of life, and it was the same stuff the rest of us want: a house and a wife and a dog.

On the same hit, we picked up the guy who owned the farm where they had been training foreign fighters. He gave us exactly nothing—we couldn't even get his name. The farms were actual farms, but they were big, so they could train the guys coming in. They had guards and were secure sites, and they taught the new guys how to use weapons and how to think like a brainwashed terrorist.

When I was in college, the Muslim Brotherhood guy who led the attack on the student government lied about it—said that I attacked him first and that there were more of us than there were of the Muslim Brotherhood guys. I asked him why he thought it was okay to lie.

"Because it's war," he said.

He had carte blanche to lie because he considered himself, as a member of the Muslim Brotherhood, at war against any "non-Muslim government," by which he meant any non-extremist-Muslim government.

When I interrogated people in Iraq, I remembered that these guys would lie to us without any remorse, and the lie would not show up on a lie detector because they felt no guilt about it.

"The worst thing you guys can do is kill me, right?" the farm owner told us. "I want to die. I'm gonna die as a martyr." If we brought him food, he said he was fasting. After three or four days, we sent him to Abu Ghraib, where they handled the high-value detainees. There was no point in keeping him. Even if he gave us information, I knew it would be false.

We caught a Libyan guy, detained him. We let him call his family. He told his brother and wife that he was going to kill himself the next day.

"Just make sure you take as many with you as you can," his wife said.

We were flabbergasted. She was not at all sad that she was about to lose her husband, and his brother wasn't sad either. This was a huge eye-opener for me: His family celebrated that he was about to give himself to the cause. It was also pointless to try to work with him—too far gone.

As I mentioned, there was no point in trying to torture information out of these guys, either—or out of anybody, period. I never saw any waterboarding while I was in Iraq, and I never heard about anyone doing it, beyond what we saw in the news. (We weren't waterboarded in training, but we did spend some time in a tub filled with ice. If people went through waterboarding training, it was to learn how bad it was. It wasn't to teach you how to do it; it was to teach you not to do it.)

I never saw any military guys torture anybody, either. When we heard about Abu Ghraib—where young soldiers had placed naked prisoners on top of one another in pyramids, walked them naked on dog leashes, and had them stand on buckets believing that if they fell off, they would be electrocuted—we were absolutely sickened.

I watched it on TV with a guy from Group—super nice guy. Greek Orthodox. He believed everybody should love everybody else but was also incredibly smart.

"Man, this is gonna be a disaster," I said to him.

"Why?" he asked.

"Dude, this is bad," I said. "This will be the best recruiting tool ever for al-Qaeda."

It felt obvious to me but not to everyone: "Look what the American occupiers, invaders, colonialists have come to do to you."

If the guys on our team were educated and had been hit with a pretty good dose of culture and still couldn't imagine the outcomes of Abu Ghraib, many of our service members were absolutely clueless. So many of us join straight from high school, having traveled only as far as the nearest football field, and we don't necessarily have a strong idea of what's going on in the world. In the United States, people tend to know US history—but not Middle Eastern history. If they know about the Crusades, it's from a Christian/ Western perspective: the Muslims are the bad guys.

But the Iraqis—and al-Qaeda—knew what the French did in Algeria: In the early 1800s, they took over land from the tribes and redistributed it to Europeans who moved there. They raped women and massacred entire villages. They desecrated cemeteries.

And they knew what the Brits did in Kenya: in 1920, they took the five million fertile acres from indigenous people and gave them to British war veterans, pushed the Kenyan people into the swamps, and essentially forced them to work for the British.

And they knew about the Crusades: a "religious" war, supported by the Roman Catholic Church, used for centuries to justify war against the much-wealthier Islamic Empire.

Al-Qaeda did not have to stretch hard to make the case that Abu Ghraib foretold of another colonization, this time by the United States.

Culturally, Abu Ghraib was offensive to me. I know that, culturally, it was offensive to most Americans, too. My friends thought of the soldiers involved in the scandal with disgust. But people in Iraq saw them as representative. After that, it was as if somebody had flipped a switch.

Before Abu Ghraib, we could go downtown, get some shawarma. You could buy stuff at the market. After Abu Ghraib, it wasn't safe. But people didn't get it.

And really, how was calling them "enemy combatants," rather than "prisoners of war," so that we could bypass the Geneva Convention—secreting people off to jail cells in Egypt and eastern Europe, as well as to Guantanamo Bay, with no legal recourse—that much different from what Saddam had done?

The insurgency swelled.

Beyond Abu Ghraib, there were outliers.

The task force worked swiftly when it came to stuff like that. However, I have no doubt that some of the task force guys pulled some shit, too—I couldn't see everybody. But what I saw was straightforward.

We didn't need to be anything else. We used classic methods: Build a relationship. Be humane. See them as humans, and make sure they see you as a human. Let them know that you're trying to help them get out of whatever bind they had put themselves in. And then let them talk.

The Moroccan kid? He just wanted to get to his family. I hope that the conversations and the compassion and the second chance mattered for that kid—that he's off being a good dad somewhere, teaching his children which mosques to avoid and telling them to do well in school.

But it didn't matter overall.

Anwar Sadat and Menachem Begin greet each for their first meeting at the Camp David Accords as Jimmy Carter and Rosalynn Carter watch on September 7, 1978. *Photo courtesy of the National Archives.*

The author kept a copy of *The New York Times* from the day Osama bin Laden was killed. *Photo courtesy of the author.*

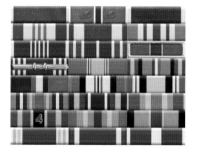

The author's rack. *Photo courtesy of the author.*

The author poses on a mission. His face has been blurred to protect his identity. *Photo courtesy of the author.*

General Stanley McChrystal, commander of NATO's International Security Assistance Force, speaks with US Army Captain Joey Nickel during a foot patrol through Muqur District in Badghis Province. *Photo by Petty Officer 1st Class Mark O'Donald, courtesy of the Defense Department.*

Operatives mess around with "disguises." *Photo courtesy of the author.*

The author sees an elephant on the hike to Kilimanjaro. *Photo courtesy of the author.*

The author takes a break from the Army—and from being shot—by hiking Mount Kilimanjaro. *Photo courtesy of the author.*

The author reaches base camp at Kilimanjaro before making the final ascent. *Photo courtesy of the author.*

ABOVE LEFT: Operatives collect intelligence from a cramped space in an undisclosed location in Africa. *Photo courtesy of the author.*

ABOVE RIGHT: Water runs brown from the taps at a hotel where the operatives lived in Africa. *Photo courtesy of the author.*

Operatives display an American flag off the coast of Africa after a successful operation. *Photo courtesy of the author.*

ABOVE: Operatives line up their vehicles in preparation for a mission. *Photo courtesy of the author.*

AT RIGHT: The author displays a company coin from the Unit. *Photo courtesy of the author.*

BELOW: US Army Special Forces assigned to Special Operations Task Force–West Haditha prepare for a mission in their area of operations in Iraq, during Operation Iraqi Freedom, August 31, 2007. *Photo courtesy of the Defense Department.*

Soldiers, marines, and airmen from US Special Operations Command Africa (SOCAF) prepare to exit a C-130J Hercules aircraft over the Malmsheim Airfield drop zone near Malmsheim, Germany, February 24, 2011. *Photo by Martin Greeson, courtesy of the Defense Department.*

The Unit's crest. *Photo courtesy of the author.*

The author (center) poses with his high school basketball team. *Photo courtesy of the author.*

The author (left) with his Boy Scout troop. *Photo courtesy of the author.*

ABOVE LEFT: The author with his brothers at the beach in Alexandria, Egypt, where he almost drowned. *Photo courtesy of the author.*

ABOVE RIGHT: The author stands with his father, who pushed hard to keep the author away from the Muslim Brotherhood. *Photo courtesy of the author.*

AT LEFT: US Special Forces continue to train troops in Ghana, as shown here. A US Army Green Beret gives a Mauritanian Special Operations soldier technical techniques to engage targets while conducting weapons training in Daboya, Ghana, March 3, 2023. The training allows African nations to share their strategies to accelerate the collective ability to adapt and overcome the terrorist threat. *Photo by Corporal Tommy L. Spitzer, courtesy of the US Army.*

US Special Operations Forces gear up for an evening mission in western Iraq. The mission resulted in the detainment of two suspected insurgents from an al-Qaeda cell believed to be responsible for planning improvised explosive device attacks, smuggling weapons, and facilitating foreign fighters. *Photo by Mass Communication Specialist 2nd Class Eli J. Medellin, courtesy of the US Navy.*

ABOVE LEFT: An advertisement, updated from the one Adam saw as a young soldier, encouraging troops to join Special Operations Forces. *Graphic by Staff Sergeant Christopher Brown, courtesy of the 5th Special Forces Group (Airborne).*

ABOVE RIGHT: Airmen assigned to the 11th Intelligence Squadron review data before a full-motion video exploitation mission on Hurlburt Field, Florida, in 2015. The 11th IS provides United States Special Operations Command and components with a focused, timely, multi-source intelligence, surveillance, and reconnaissance capability for special operations forces worldwide. *Photo by Airmain Kai White, courtesy of the US Air Force.*

Green Berets of 3rd Special Forces Group (Airborne) perform a nighttime free-fall jump at ten thousand feet in 2021 at Fort Bragg, North Carolina. *Photo by Specialist Garrett Whitfield, courtesy of the 3rd Brigade Combat Team, 82nd Airborne Division.*

Major Ryan Collins (right), the 1st Special Forces Group (Airborne) signal officer, and Staff Sergeant Robert Carter, a satellite communications operator, troubleshoot a satellite antenna during a training exercise in 2018. Collins was awarded the Army Special Operations Forces Communicator of the Year Award for significant contributions toward the special operations force mission of providing command, control, communications, computers, and intelligence (C4I) support in both garrison and tactical environments. *Photo by Specialist Austin Pope, courtesy of the 1st Special Forces Group (Airborne).*

US Army General Stanley A. McChrystal, commander of NATO's International Security Assistance Force and US Forces-Afghanistan, addresses Marines of the 2nd Battalion, 2nd Marine Regiment at Combat Outpost Sharp in the Garmsir District of Helmand Province in 2010. *Photo by Petty Officer 1st Class Mark O'Donald, courtesy of the US Navy.*

Adam poses in front of Saddam Hussein's "Victory Arch," which commemorates the Iran-Iraq War, in central Baghdad. *Photo courtesy of the author.*

Adam and his team wait as a flock of MH-6M Little Birds and their occupants prepare to take out a terrorist using information gained by Adam and his team. *Photo courtesy of the author.*

AT LEFT: Many of Adam's experiences feel surreal, including conducting a mission as a giraffe surveils his team. *Photo courtesy of the author.*

BELOW: Wild ostriches operate in the savanna as Adam and his team work nearby. *Photo courtesy of the author.*

Adam stayed in this building, the Tikrit palace complex, or Hussein's "Green Palace," while in Iraq. *Photo courtesy of the author.*

Saddam had lions in his houses as pets. The Unit found them starving to death after Saddam escaped. *Photo courtesy of the author.*

ABOVE: Adam (right) and his boss prepare to go out on a mission. *Photo courtesy of the author.*

AT RIGHT: Adam and his team use local vehicles and methods to transport their equipment. *Photo courtesy of the author.*

A surveillance mission tracking an al-Qaeda cell—the tourists are operatives from the author's team. *Photo courtesy of the author.*

Adam (left) and his team prepare equipment in their living quarters while deployed. *Photo courtesy of the author.*

Sweet █████

For all the days I was not present for you, I was fighting to make sure that you have the best life a father can give his most precious love, his daughter.

I love you with all my heart and you can always count on me.

And for all the days you missed me, you deserve this
Bronze Star (OEF: 2007-2008)

Daddy (█████)

1 April █████

ABOVE: The bronze star Adam earned in 2006 and presented to his daughter for her service when he retired. *Photo courtesy of the author.*

AT LEFT: Adam poses with his daughters after his retirement ceremony in 2016. *Photo courtesy of the author.*

I JOINED THE ARMY so I wouldn't have to drive for a living.

But when I went to Iraq the second time, driving a local stolen yellow car provided the perfect cover in the continued search for Saddam Hussein. It was hard for the six-foot-tall, square-jawed white guys to fit in—even with beards and keffiyehs. But I could sneak out, and there was a Hawaiian soldier who could be like a chameleon. I took her out a lot with me in the local car. She'd cover up, and no one could tell what nationality she was.

I'd drive out into the city, and since an Egyptian company was building the Iraqi phone system, many people just assumed I worked for the phone company, which became a good story for me. I visited some internet cafés and built a good rapport with the owners. The cafés were used by extremists at the time, and some

of the owners were extremists, as well. One café owner even let me fix his equipment. That probably wasn't his best move.

It could be terrifying—if the café owner had seen my stolen local car while I was pretending to be an IT dude, I was going to have some explaining to do.

By then, there was so much anger. This was our fault.

I could see this from the driver's seat, hear it when I went out on the streets. If people think you're a driver, they'll say things they won't say in front of someone they're trying to impress or hide things from. With me around, they talked about the day-to-day. From the base, surrounded by concrete walls and concertina wire, it was hard to have a good idea of what life looked like to the average Iraqi.

It's funny, when you think about it, but everyone makes the joke about how armies know how to break things. But our previous, recent-ish missions—Bosnia, Kosovo—had been about peace-keeping: about rebuilding and mediating and helping people feel safe. But in Iraq, for some reason, all of that got tossed away. We'd just break everything. We'd break the government. We'd break the infrastructure. We'd break the justice system. People with knowledge—the lawyers and doctors and scientists and musicians and oil technicians and bankers and politicians and government officials—feared for their lives and fled.

There are things I am proud of about our work in Iraq. But there were some serious failures, too. Our goal as a nation su-perseded the needs of the people. Our Middle East experts in the United States were absolutely ignored, and everything they predicted came to pass. Their predictions came down to this: Saddam is a bad man. Without Saddam or a strong replacement,

the country will fall into tribal and religious warfare. That's exactly what happened, only worse, because not only did we remove Saddam but we removed every semblance of structure from the country.

When we destroyed their infrastructure at the beginning of the war, we destroyed everyday life. As I drove around the city, I could see it at the most basic level. In Iraq, traffic lights were controlled by a police officer—someone stood there and flipped a switch. When the police were gone, traffic became chaos. But that police officer also no longer got paid. Did the guy work for Hussein? Peripherally, yes, and so did everybody else, and nobody had a choice. I would say 50 percent of the guys in Hussein's Baath Party did not have a choice. So now they were blacklisted. They weren't allowed to hold jobs, but there was no one to replace them. No one else had been trained to cover government jobs or to administer those jobs.

The guy who handled passport distribution and renewal? Gone. Not only that, but with no one to guard the building, someone took home the passport machine and started making passports. Egyptian guys were suddenly Iraqi citizens, for a small fee of $50.

The guy who controlled the deeds for property ownership? He took his computer and files and went home. If you liked your neighbor's house, you'd give that guy a bribe, and it was yours—houses that had been in families for generations suddenly belonged to somebody else. We heard complaints from three or four people at a time all claiming the same house—and all with documents to prove it.

Driver's licenses? No one there. Machine to make them? Someone's backyard.

That's what I drove out into during the day: chaos.

After I came back from my mission, I had to drive back on base. That terrified me more than driving the streets, going into internet cafés, or getting caught in some bit of bullshit in my cover story. Your average soldier at the gate may have been looking for a reason to pull the trigger, and an Iraqi local yellow car barreling toward the gate provided one.

Every time I went out, I would stop at the gate.

"Hey. I'm going out," I'd say. "I'm one of the good guys. Please don't shoot me when I come back in."

On my way back, I would call ahead: "Hey. It's the American guy in the local yellow car. I'm on my way back in. Please don't shoot me."

Then I would place bright-orange panels on the front of the taxi so they could see me from far away.

During the day, we'd do surveillance and gather intel, and then at night, we'd go out with other elite units' guys, looking for people associated with Saddam: relatives, drivers, security.

Just as in Bosnia, I didn't get a lot of sleep.

One night, we thought we had him.

Well, they thought we had him.

Saddam.

Again.

A lot of the CIA guys came to Iraq to get their feet wet, so their case officers were coming straight out of school. They had no experience whatsoever, and they'd just graduated from a course that made them think they were smarter than everybody else on the planet. The Iraqi guys played them hard.

The CIA had a female interpreter who didn't know I also spoke Arabic. So when she translated during interrogations, she would tweak whatever was said a bit to support whatever her position was. There were four of us, me and three guys attached to the task force, as part of a larger group going after Saddam. When she translated, they'd ask me what really happened. When she found out, she cursed me out.

I saw warlords play the CIA guys—for instance, some elementary-school-educated guy in Africa or Afghanistan or Pakistan would play a CIA guy for a year. All the while, the CIA guy would be thinking, *I've got that guy in my back pocket.* But the local guy used his street smarts to get his money without having to give up anything of value.

I ended up being in a position of authority, in part because I was Muslim. I was the right guy at the right time. I was the only guy in the room who had any cultural understanding of Iraq, so people listened to me. But I was thinking, *Maybe there should be more than one person? Maybe Harvard shouldn't be your only feeder school?*

But this time, our guys were sure they had found Hussein, on the basis of information from one guy.

We rode in a convoy of three or four cars, and there were four guys in my car. Just me from our side, and everybody else was from other elite Army units. A source had told us that Saddam Hussein was in the town we were going to.

"Man, that guy's lying to you," I told everyone. "He's not really a good guy."

"Well, he passed the polygraph."

Right.

And off we went.

One of the task force operators was driving, and everybody was amped. Or amped-ish, in my case, because I was pretty sure the source was lying.

Another operator in the back said, "Man, I really wish we could listen to 'Highway to Hell.'"

And all of a sudden, the song came on. Everybody laughed. Crazy. What a coincidence.

One of the other guys said, "Man, you're so lucky. I wish we could listen to 'You Shook Me All Night Long.'" And it totally came on.

That's insane. What are the chances of that?

Anyone who has served in Iraq knows they're not supposed to listen to music on patrol. And anyone who has served in Iraq has also seen helmeted heads in a Humvee nodding along to Drowning Pool.

"Okay, but wouldn't it be nuts if the next song was 'Bulls on Parade'?"

"Come wit' it now."

"Fuck, every time you like a song, it comes up!" the driver said.

Somebody had the precursor to something like the iPod, of course, and was controlling the music. To be fair, it was 2004, and he was a smart guy, but the technology was new, and it was way over his head. We all had a hell of a time laughing at him. We needed a way to enjoy the long ride.

We went to a base outside town to spend the night until sunrise.

Our guys were in these big meat trucks and in team trucks, while we were in nice BMWs. We stormed the heck out of the house.

We did not find Saddam.

We did not find explosive devices and booby traps and guards everywhere, as our polygraph-proof source said we would.

We did find an old farmer, his wife and son, and some little kids.

And we found important electronic devices: an Atari video game. That thing was probably worth a fortune.

In 1989.

"I told you."

Our task force commander got so sick of us being played that he took the informant to the family and said, "This is the guy who told us Saddam was in your house."

The other agencies complained and said that he was also their source and that people were threatening to kill him.

Bummer.

I liked that task force commander—he was a straightforward guy.

We detained innocent people because of that source, and we risked our own lives. He put that farmer's life at risk. He just wanted his thousand bucks for offering up information. Probably sixty to seventy of our hits were based on bad information from bad sources. We were so naive in the beginning.

Way too often, people would rat out their neighbors over some beef they had that didn't involve harboring fugitives or hiding weapons or plotting against the government.

The old guy looked like somebody's great-grandfather. We took them all back to Baghdad, and all of us were upset about the mission—disappointed and demoralized.

We went back to where we were staying, one of the palaces in the Green Zone. More mosaics and murals and gold on everything.

Rooms had been partitioned off to the point that it had started to look more like an office building filled with cubicles rather than a palace, but the entrance was still grand.

As we settled in for the night, the task force commander came in to chat with us.

"What do you think of the older guy?" he asked me.

"We never should have taken him," I said. I explained the situation to him.

"That older farmer, his reputation and his pride are incredibly important to him," I said. "And by disrespecting him, his kids will come after us. And his grandkids will come after us. We just pissed off his entire village."

We talked some more and tried to figure out how to release the guy back home while also giving him back his dignity.

That commander was solid.

When we went out at night, we never knew what we'd encounter. We didn't know if they were going to try to blow us up or shoot us, and so we were scared. And then we'd bust in, after midnight, and it would be all shock-and-awe, like George Bush said, and then we'd handcuff everybody and put them on their knees and interrogate them.

We did that to men and women.

I remember telling another one of the guys, "Man, imagine that's your mom."

The guy next to her? Kneeling on the ground watching her be interrogated? That's her son. And we just turned him into a terrorist, because the next opportunity he gets to shoot you, he's going to shoot you.

I remember going in with some of the young Ranger guys

and wondering if they were thinking things through carefully—if they were thinking about the big mission. A lady at one house kept telling us that one of them stole a gun. The Iraqis were allowed, by our rules, to have a gun to protect their houses and their families—it was a war zone, after all.

"Listen," I said to her, "my guys didn't steal your gun." I spent several minutes defending them.

As it turns out, one of those clowns had stolen her fucking gun.

We used different methods to narrow down where we thought Hussein might be, but we needed an exact location. All of us tried to think in different ways about where Saddam might be. But I wondered if we were maybe thinking too far outside the box. So where would I go if I were on the run from the world's greatest military? Strike that: Where would I go if I were Saddam Hussein and on the run from the world's greatest military?

Well. We knew Saddam trusted few people. We knew that some Iraqis were willing to rat out even innocent people to make some cash. So, if I were Saddam in a bind, I would go where people loved me.

"He's in Tikrit," I said. "That's his hometown. They're hardcore in love with him up there—they write poetry about the guy."

It was a gut feeling.

They divided us up: half of us went to Tikrit, and half of us went to Mosul. Smith, a blond guy of Scottish descent, went with me to Tikrit. He was like the paparazzi—just constantly taking photos.

"Someday, you're going to appreciate this," he told me. He could also smoke the heck out of me running.

Soldiers started interrogating Hussein's family.

"Yup, he's at my farm," one guy the Army had detained said. "He's in a hole. I'll show you guys where he's at."

So we ended up finding Saddam by using strategy rather than informants.

"Can I have the $25 million?" the guy with the hole on his farm asked.

"No," the Army said. "You didn't volunteer that information; you got detained."

He didn't get shit.

I left Iraq the week before they found Saddam.

I was pissed.

I mean, I was thrilled that they found Saddam Hussein.

I was pissed I wasn't there for it.

SEVENTEEN   THE MOUTH OF THE RIVER

I DIDN'T WANT TO be in Iraq or Afghanistan, though I spent time in both places. I wanted to be in Africa. I wanted to go after the guys who had interfered with my childhood in Egypt, who had bombed the embassies while I was stationed in Germany, and who had attacked both my country and my faith on September 11.

If you wanted glory, you raised your hand for Iraq or Afghanistan. There, you could walk in the door, say hello, and walk out with a Bronze Star. I wasn't that guy—and neither were a few of my teammates.

Even with all those deployments to Iraq and Afghanistan to mop up the mess, the floor kept getting wet. And we dried it. And then it would get wet. And then we would dry it.

Hey, dumbasses: Where's the water coming from?

Africa. If we blocked the water at the source in Africa, it would prevent little rivulets from spreading to Iraq or Afghanistan.

Or New York.

But nobody wanted to go to Africa, because they worried about the prevalence of HIV, malaria, and Ebola. (Guys will run into gunfire, but tell them they might bleed from their eyeballs and assholes, and it's a no-go.)

I am African, originally. Africa felt personal. And it felt personal to me to let my Unit headquarters know that I didn't just want the easy missions where I spoke the language. If some of my people were causing problems, I wanted to take care of it—and I could. If I could get someone to sit down and talk with me in East and West Africa, then I wasn't just an operative who knows Arabic. I was the complete package. The local people trusted me enough to let me lead their prayers.

Killing one innocent man is like killing all mankind.

Culture may seem simple—like something a person could Google or read a book about. Military leaders seemed to think language training was enough. It wasn't. There are anecdotes and nuances and cultural references and poems that everyone memorizes in first grade. A soldier might learn not to show an Arabic man the sole of his shoe because it's disrespectful, but so would any tourist who closely reads his travel guide. And it's just one thing.

I mean, think about all the things Americans get offended about.

You could compare it to growing up in the North versus growing up in the South. A New York City kid probably won't do well in the swamp, and a kid who grew up fishing in the Everglades may not do so well in Central Park. Students may learn in business school that they have to be honest and straightforward, but they may operate in a country where bribery is not just the norm; it's expected. In the Middle East, people don't just name a price; they haggle it. But you can't lump in all the Arabs together, either. There are twenty different countries with twenty different cultures and twenty different languages and twenty different religions. If I go to a Shia mosque, I take a small rock and put it on the ground in front of me. When I pray, my forehead touches that rock. Sunnis don't do that. And there's more than one kind of Shia and more than one kind of Sunni.

For those who grew up in the Middle East or northern Africa, these things are second nature.

There are Arabs who eat with their hands, but you would never see an Arab in a city eat that way. Once when I was in an African country, they brought a big plate of food. I used a spoon, and everybody laughed at my inability to eat with my hands. But instead of being offended, they expected it because they knew I was a city boy—from Africa.

Depending on where you are in Africa, you won't just shake hands; you'll perform anything from a triple hand maneuver to, in Egypt, a light handshake and a kiss on the cheek.

In the Gulf, you don't shake hands. You touch shoulders. In Saudi Arabia, they touch noses. It may take a minute for a football player from Minnesota to manage a nose touch with a guy in a "man dress."

The guys in the Unit were successful because they were good observers and apt learners—but I wanted to use my innate skill set. I wanted to show headquarters why diversity in the Unit was important.

I felt as if we could make more of a difference in Africa. The guys arriving in Iraq and Afghanistan from Africa had been brainwashed already—and they were ready to die for their cause. The extremists from Saudi Arabia didn't want to die. They wanted to go back and tell their peeps, "I'm a hero. I was just in Iraq."

"Don't send me Muslims from the Gulf," Abu Musab al-Zarqawi once said in an intercepted message. "Send me Muslims from Africa. They are ready to die." Zarqawi was the mastermind behind what is now known as ISIS.

We had to stop the flow.

In Africa, we fought ideology—the source of the river. Along the way, we tracked the people spreading the ideology, and we mopped.

The authoritarian leaders in the Middle East and Africa had invited in that ideology by adopting the mindset of the British colonialists: I'm going to educate you only enough that I can control you. Savages can't be controlled, but I won't educate you to the point that you are smarter than I am or that you realize I am taking advantage of you.

Yeah, it happened in the States, too.

Say a shepherd gets a big dog to help with his flock. He feeds the dog well because he doesn't want the dog to eat the sheep. But he keeps the sheep stupid so the dog, who's happy because he's being fed well, can control them. That's many countries in a nutshell: security forces with a lot of bribery built in, guarding people who don't know how to get over the fence.

Some Arab leaders still think this way. It means their people can easily be convinced by extremists, too, because they haven't learned how to think. In some countries, twenty-four seven, the media broadcast the accomplishments of the current ruler. They do not broadcast human rights violations, protests, the number of people dying from COVID-19. It's not that "the Saudis don't have enough freedom" so much as that the Saudis don't have the form of education they need to think critically about the world.

The government does not encourage analytical or critical thinking. This is why things got nuts when they suddenly said, after one hundred years of saying the opposite, "Just kidding. A woman driving a car is not haram."

I was at a conference in Saudi Arabia recently—after I retired from the military. I took an Uber to the conference center.

"Hey," the Saudi driver said, "so what's going on in there?"

"It's an IT conference," I said.

"Yeah," he said, "but what exactly is going on?"

"Companies come in, and they talk about IT," I said. "It's pretty nerdy."

"I thought it was a whorehouse," he said.

"Wait, why?"

"I saw women go inside naked."

The naked women? They were fully dressed, but their abayas— those flowing black robes women wear over their clothes in Saudi Arabia—were open. And he could see their faces.

This was a young man. He lacked the ability to think critically, so he leaped from open abaya to whorehouse.

Education in the Middle East focuses on whether you should enter a bathroom with your left foot or right foot first. (Your left, if you're keeping track.) That can lead to a three-hour discussion about who's going to get to heaven. But they're never going to make it to the moon.

(I have to give kudos to the United Arab Emirates, who made it to Mars by focusing on education and progressive thought.)

When I arrived in Africa, four guys had already been sent to the Horn of Africa—the first four there. Four white guys. Three operatives and an officer. Three of them were crazy smart. They were not given any information; they just went. They started looking at what was there and generally tried to figure out what might work, from technical and operational perspectives. Then they started to build. They recommended we create a mission there, and our higher command gave us some areas of responsibility and started sending in more people.

I came in the second round in early 2004—right after my second tour in Iraq.

We figured out which extremist groups were getting trained where and then followed them from there. The foreign fighters were more likely to head to Iraq than Afghanistan.

We wanted to know where people were becoming radicalized.

A lot of these guys weren't al-Qaeda yet, but they wanted to be, which made them dangerous because they needed to convince al-Qaeda that they were crazy enough to qualify—as if they were joining a violent gang. They kidnapped people; European nurses were among the targets.

In 2004, we focused on East Africa. We realized that the foreign fighters coming to Iraq and Afghanistan were coming from Africa. They were transported through the deserts, to Somalia. Then they'd cross the Red Sea. Some of those guys went a long fucking way from Algeria, Morocco, or Mali to Iraq to fight, and when they got there, they found they were still in a better situation than they had been at home. We weren't fighting local thugs. We were fighting an ideology being used to recruit desperate guys. Those guys, they were born into poverty: They didn't have a way out. They didn't have the right to dream.

It made them easy to recruit.

Somalia was al-Qaeda's biggest training area after the war started in Afghanistan. In the 1950s and 1960s, Egypt built schools in Somalia to teach Arabic and try to expand the Arab world. Somalis saw Egyptians as scholars—as experts on Islam. Who then came marching in on a wave of violent cassette tapes? The Muslim Brotherhood. Somalia was ripe for it.

As part of our mission, we tracked guys who traveled to Somalia and then left through neighboring countries without anyone ever knowing they had been in Somalia. Some of them were US citizens.

We started building a target deck: Who were the real players? We started digging into the embassy bombings in Kenya and Tanzania.

All the targets were connected. We operated from Africa, but we tracked these guys everywhere. We had guys in more than twenty-seven countries at one time. People from every unit made up the team—not just my Unit guys.

Over the years, we went from a four-man team to a large task force. But that four-man team created the right conditions for the task force.

I was excited—ready, motivated, determined—when I went to Africa.

And those first guys already in Africa? They would welcome me as any Oakley-wearing operative would: by reminding me that prayer is better than sleep.

THE THREE GUYS ALREADY in-country picked me up from the airport when I first arrived. I had no idea of the basics: housing, food, transportation. They set up everything—handed me an envelope with a hundred dollars in local currency, a phone with a local number, and a gun. Finally, they gave me a tour of the town.

"Why does it smell like everything's on fire?" I asked.

"Burning trash," they said. "Get used to it."

Then they took me to our apartment. They gave me a nice room that overlooked the city.

"You'll enjoy it," they said with weird smiles on their faces.

And they left.

It was a Saturday. Sunday morning, at 6:00 a.m., I heard . . . singing?

Except it was like some kind of Lorelei or *En-Naddāha* bullshit—like sirens or genies calling me to my death. Or like someone had already died and the city was wailing. It was eerie.

A church stood across the street, and they broadcast, through bullhorns, prayers in the local language at dawn.

"How'd you sleep?" my friends asked.

"You motherfuckers."

"Nope, you're the new guy," they said, laughing. "That's your initiation. Tonight, you're buying us drinks."

I owed them—in more ways than one. These were the guys who first recognized the stream of Muslim extremists flowing from the Horn of Africa, across the Red Sea, over Saudi Arabia, and into Iraq. It was essentially a smuggling operation, and it seemed like a good place to focus.

"We believe there's enough activity here that we need to set up a mission."

They weren't strangers: one of them I had gone through selection with.

I'm sure he got a new glass eye after selection—that thing must have been cracked as hell after the interrogator knocked it out.

My wife says I have a GPS system in my brain, but it's nothing like what Jacob had going on. He knew the whole town inside out. He made sure I knew where the British embassy was, in case of emergency—there was some kind of agreement. He showed me the US embassy. Then he showed me how to get to where we would be working. He told me where I could go for food, as well as where I couldn't. Some places were targets.

Because he had one eye, Jacob had to tilt his head to look at things. As he drove, I thought to myself, *How in the fuck do you know all this stuff?* He'd only been there a month. If he knew we needed two routes to go to work, he would find five. Different hours. Different cars. Different roads.

He named his equipment after good-looking women so that when we talked over the phone about moving gear, an eavesdropper would think we were talking about girls.

He could go with the flow with anyone.

"Are you Canadian?" someone in town might ask.

"Yup," he'd say. "Beekeeper."

Apparently, there are a lot of Canadian beekeepers in Africa. He could make up a story in the split of a second. He could do anything.

Sal was the technical brain. He could run collections out of a brown bag. He also fixed collection equipment as easily as a chef can chop tomatoes, but he could do it blindfolded. He'd stay on the phone with me for hours and be like, "That green button? Turn it to the right." I'd say, "Are you looking at the same thing as I am?" "No," he'd say, "it's in my head." He was that good.

There were two guys who went in and out of Africa more than anybody else: Brandon and Tim.

Tim and I already spoke Swahili: Tim spoke like a native; I was just able to get by. But Brandon needed to learn. I took him to Zanzibar and dropped him off for a month with a Swahili teacher. When I picked him up, he spoke it almost like a local. When I went to Zanzibar afterward, everyone talked about how nice Brandon was—he could have run for mayor.

Tim had a mind for languages, too. He learned Spanish and French from books, while also speaking Arabic and Swahili. He had the most innovative mind I've ever encountered, but everybody loved him. He was the smoothest operator.

We flowed in and out, operatives from each military branch. The SEALs started coming around 2005 or 2006, and by 2009, there were more than one hundred people working the Africa mission. I estimate we stopped between thirty and forty terrorist attacks in the United States alone and at least fifty terrorist attacks worldwide.

I was in Africa, on and off, from 2003 to 2009. I deployed for about three months at a time, but there wasn't a "usually," beyond that my wife usually didn't know when I'd be home.

In Africa, we looked for clues everywhere.

Before they smuggled terrorists, the traffickers smuggled tobacco, drugs, and prostitutes and other humans. All of a sudden, their mission changed—and it was even better: *If I smuggle extremists, people think I'm a good Muslim.*

Really, they just wanted the money.

We kept connecting dots.

We learned things that surprised me.

When we—and just about every other country—change our border guards, we relieve in place, which means the guard doesn't leave a post until the replacement guard arrives. It's a big-enough deal that it's one of the US military's general orders: "I will not quit my post until properly relieved."

But early on during the war in Iraq, somehow we learned that Syria's guards, after finishing their shifts, simply left their posts—and their replacements showed up about fifteen minutes later. Fifteen minutes when no one manned the border. Foreign fighters would go to Syria, spend a few weeks there while they obtained fake Iraqi passports, and then come across the border saying that they were Iraqis who had fled the country during the war.

Those fifteen-minute gaps? That was intentional. That's how they smuggled in the fighters.

We had a target—a guy who was smuggling people. He brought people all the way from Chechnya, as well as Africa, Bosnia, Morocco, Sudan, Egypt, and Saudi Arabia. Saudis tended to go to Syria for summer vacation—as the kid from Morocco had done—so it was easy for them to get there. (They weren't necessarily there to kill Brits or Americans. They were looking for Shia Muslims.) Our target would switch out a Saudi Arabian guy's passport for a fake Iraqi passport. Dude took twenty-five Saudi Arabian guys into Iraq—and then lost their passports. When they got back to Syria, they couldn't go home because they only had their Iraqi passports.

We eventually got him. The US military killed him at the end of the Bush administration. His father was also killed in the attack.

We went in on the ground to some countries to get information. We had to be creative.

One day, three of us sat in the garden of one of our small houses in Africa and thought about how we could solve that problem. We couldn't get to some locations: locations with terrorist training camps, towns run by al-Qaeda. We came up with a design for some equipment, ensured it was idiotproof.

Jacob immediately gave this piece of equipment a name.

Now some other agencies use this invention of ours.

That's why the promotions in the Unit are so fast. I always felt humbled being around those guys. *Why didn't I think of that?* It was hard to be the dumbest guy in the room.

Lucas learned Arabic in four months.

His Arabic must be fucked up, I thought. I kept testing him. If we were watching something, I'd say, "Hey, Lucas. What are we watching?"

"It's a sitcom," he'd say.

"What did they just say?" I'd ask.

And he'd tell me the whole plotline.

This motherfucker's a genius.

I had read an article that said very smart people have big heads—they need them for their big brains. Lucas had a really big head.

"Hey, Lucas," I said. "What's your helmet size?" I didn't know it was a touchy subject for him. The military did not have a helmet that would fit him.

"Man, that's why you speak five languages," I said.

"Shut the fuck up, man," he said.

We had a team sergeant, Dean, who looked like Elton John. He was not tall—but he was wicked strong. After talking to him for a bit, I'd have to pull out my phone to look up words. He went to Ranger school in his forties and passed the first time. It just didn't seem as if anything was hard for him. But he was a great listener. He was strategic about where he sent us, playing to our strengths and weaknesses rather than just trying to fill slots.

I was extremely lucky to have him. And he just happened to be the guy who recruited me to the Unit.

One of the guys was in a band. Another was a graphic designer. He joined the Army when he was seventeen, and then he retired when he was thirty-seven, went to college, worked for DC Comics or something, and then came back. Super artistic.

Why the fuck are you here?

During one mission in Africa, in the middle of fucking nowhere, I woke up early to the sound of beautiful piano music. The people we'd rented the house from had left a piano. I went downstairs, and there was this Ranger at the keys.

"Dude, when did you learn how to play piano?" I asked.

"Here," he said.

Right. He's a killer, but he loves to play the piano.

Surrounded by brilliance, I was there to prove myself. I didn't want to be a one-trick pony. Yeah, I could speak Arabic. When I was growing up, that didn't make me special. But technically, I'm good. I could get information in ways other than just understanding the language: I could get it from technical means. I could get it from human means. I could get it from different sources. I could learn another language. And I could memorize anything.

We deployed with different guys each time. After a while, I knew whom I clicked with, and we loved to deploy together. One of my favorites also became a senior—we were both team leaders—so we didn't get to deploy together, but we'd replace each other and meet coming and going. We'd work to make the handover last as long as possible because we enjoyed it so much.

Generally, we got to choose our operatives. We usually had an analyst on each trip, but we had no say in whom that would be. They were all sharp. We did have some leverage because we could send them home if they screwed up or had a conflict with someone on the team. Usually, the threat of a return ticket home was enough to fix the issue.

We went wherever the Army needed us. If we were tracking bad guys and they popped up in Timbuktu, then that's where we went. But a group of us stayed on the pulse of East Africa. This small group constantly briefed everybody else about what was going on so that, even when we were not deployed, we knew what needed to be done. We didn't miss a beat when we went back—always knew who the new players were and where the power struggles were and who was sleeping with whose wife and who was trying to stab somebody else in the back.

Days of Our Lives, Unit-style.

Al-Qaeda is just like any other dysfunctional organization. There might have been a smart, well-educated guy, but he wasn't as strong as the thug. There were guys who were so smart we knew we'd never catch them. They simply did not leave a trace. They planned everything. But the alpha guy wasn't necessarily the smart guy. In al-Shabaab, in Somalia, the thug was in charge.

We had no choice but to work well together—we never knew what we would encounter.

In one country, we often felt as if we were being followed.

We were, generally speaking.

But once, we were driving—to lunch or work or a meeting with a source—and a car in front of us started swerving back and forth.

That seems bad.

We looked behind us to make sure no one was acting up on the other end. *Is this guy trying to harass us?* Back and forth, back and forth. *Is he trying to block us?* We figured the best way to deal with the situation was to get out of the situation—and to figure out if we were even part of the situation.

We pulled up next to the car, using the defensive-driving techniques we had been taught.

Back and forth, back and forth.

And we laughed.

The man drove with one hand. In that hand, he also had a chunk of khat—basically a stimulant that's popular in some areas of the Middle East and Africa that's made from twigs from a shrub. Every time he wanted another bite of khat, he turned the wheel so the drug was near his mouth, tore a chunk off with his teeth, and then turned the wheel back.

Back and forth.

Here we were, all paranoid because we were in the kind of place that makes you paranoid, and this fucker was just trying to get a hit.

Another time, we flew from the capital to a coastal city to go after a target. One of their guys got into our aircraft, sat on the floor, and pulled out a bag of khat.

"Hey, what's going on?" the pilot asked. "He's sitting on the floor and using drugs on a US aircraft?"

"You want to tell him?" I asked. "If he wants to sit on the floor, he can sit on the floor. We're going to go, we're going to detain some guys, and we're gonna call it a day." We learned to pick our battles.

During my travels in northern Africa, I found the same hateful cassette tapes I had heard as a child in Alexandria.

Those hateful messages could lead to dangerous days for us.

We were once in a country in the Middle East, tracking training camps and so on, and we went to a small city on the Red Sea—there were four of us. Of course, we didn't have Google

Maps, so we were running on Garmin. We had a general idea of where we were—a point on a map—but not the "what" of where we were. We ended up on a tiny street, and we had no choice but to continue down that street.

All of a sudden, we were surrounded by AK-47s, rocket-propelled grenades, and grenades laid out on tables for sale.

Shit.

I drove. The guy sitting next to me was Mexican American, so he could pass. The guy in the back, Sonny, was Italian American, so he could pass. But Deacon? Deacon was six feet, five inches and blond.

"Deacon. Get the fuck down."

He slumped down as much as a six-foot-five dude can just as we approached a checkpoint. This was not a government checkpoint. This was an illegal weapons dealer checkpoint.

There were kiosks filled with handguns, Russian weapons, helmets, military uniforms. And about halfway through, we hit the checkpoint in the middle.

"What are you guys doing here?" the guy at the checkpoint asked, in Arabic. I mean, I can easily pass for an Arab, but maybe not someone who should have been in that market.

"I'm just an Egyptian guy," I said. "I work for the phone company. I think we're lost."

"Yes," he said. "You are."

But the street was too small for a U-turn.

"Can we just keep going?" I asked.

"Let me get you to the other side," he said.

He jumped up on the running board, arm slung through the

window holding on to the grab handle, Deacon huddled down in the back seat holding his breath.

We drove about half a mile like that, him chatting with people along the way.

"Yeah, yeah—they got lost."

We got to the end, and he gave us directions.

I didn't think we were going to live through that one.

The work could feel frustrating just because of the sheer numbers of people we saw bleeding from that source—wave after wave of young people. If we took out one access point, another would sprout. And this was a long-term mission. We weren't going to head off the source in one deployment or even one decade. We were patient. We had been trained for it. Slowly, we began to see some progress in the form of evidence, people willing to work with us, and we gained a better understanding of how the network flowed.

Beginning in 2003, we had started work to find the guys who carried out the two embassy attacks in 1998. There were several people involved, but we determined that Fahid Mohammed Ally Msalam, along with Sheikh Ahmed Salim Swedan, both originally from Kenya, bought the trucks used for the bombings in both Kenya and Tanzania. Msalam was charged with 213 counts of murder and was al-Qaeda's operations chief in Pakistan. Swedan was his sidekick and was also indicted. They were also responsible for an assassination attempt on Benazir Bhutto, the former prime minister of Pakistan, who was killed when a man shot her after a rally and then detonated his suicide vest.

But most importantly, Msalam and Swedan had been training

others to do the same. On New Year's Day, 2009, an unmanned CIA drone allegedly killed them both at an al-Qaeda safe house in Pakistan.[18] Msalam was the one we wanted. He was a logistics whiz and probably the top African al-Qaeda guy when he was killed.

In 2020, the United States negotiated a settlement with Sudan to pay millions to compensate victims and their families in those bombings, including both Americans and people from other countries.

Full circle.

But there were a lot of fucking circles.

---

18 Randall Mikkelsen, "Qaeda Pakistan Leader Believed Dead: U.S. Official," Reuters, January 8, 2009, https://www.reuters.com/article/us-security-usa-pakistan-idUSTRE50807R20090109.

NINETEEN

A FRIEND AND I once went to Abu Dhabi, where there are wide walkways along the water, a beautiful skyline, a palace, malls, and one of the most gorgeous mosques I've ever seen: the Sheikh Zayed Mosque. It gleams, purely white with gold details, and all of the arches and rounded ceilings and keyhole cutouts create something that feels like an intricate puzzle.

"Will they let me in?" he asked. A Jewish man in a mosque?

While we were inside, we passed a group of monks.

Religion played out in an interesting way on the team.

The three or four guys who traveled with me in Africa—my team—didn't necessarily see me pray, but they saw a prayer rug in my room. I'm pretty sure everyone was praying on those missions.

I'm also sure that, to them, it seemed as if I was always fasting—

the whole month for Ramadan. But some of the guys fasted with me for support—or because they wanted to lose weight. They'd often try to adjust the time of mission because they knew I hadn't eaten.

"Man, you're starving," they'd tease. "We don't want to see you hungry. You're going to die."

If there had been a reason to break my fast, I would have. Religion is meant to help people, not hurt them.

But I didn't necessarily broadcast to the bigger team that I was Muslim.

My friend also didn't let on that he was Jewish. It was enough of a thing that it was hard to know who would react negatively and how that would affect your ability to do your job. Some people don't even put it on their dog tags, which is a big deal because that's how the Army knows how to bury your ass.

Sometimes, not saying I was Muslim allowed me to gauge who might not work well with Muslims in other countries. But I also wanted people to see me for me, rather than as "that Muslim guy."

Interestingly, when people learned I was Muslim, some people tended to feel more comfortable opening up about themselves— other minorities, women, gay people. They probably figured if I didn't tell people I was Muslim, I probably wasn't going to run around saying, "Sally's a lesbian."

I wasn't just a minority—I was a triple minority. I'm a minority religion. I'm a minority race. And I'm a first-generation immigrant.

I served with a female soldier—awesome, sweet, gorgeous. So of course, everyone wanted to date her. She came to my house and played with my kids, and she was great with them.

"You really need to find somebody," I said, thinking she'd be a great mom.

"I found somebody," she said.

Sweet!

"Wow," I said. "He's a lucky guy because you're gorgeous and awesome."

"No," she said. "She's a lucky woman."

Anytime you can make people in your group feel more comfortable—by building trust—the group will be stronger. That's awfully hard to do if people feel as if they have to keep secrets because so few others are like them. We're missing out on talent and trust by sticking with the good ol' boys' club.

Dubai's an interesting place because it markets itself as a company would. The people in charge care about what outsiders think of them—mostly because they care about their brand. But still.

In 2019, the United Arab Emirates promoted the "Year of Tolerance," which maybe isn't the first thing you think of when you think Middle East. They talked about coexistence and respect.

My Jewish friend and I used to hang out in Dubai a lot, either between trips or when we needed some R and R. We would be coming from someplace in the Middle East where the women were covered from head to toe and the men were involved in terrorist training camps, and then we'd land in Dubai, and it would be like landing on a different planet. We'd go to the beach in the morning, and there would be a woman in full hijab walking along the shore. And walking near her would be a woman in a bikini.

Everybody was cool; everybody was coexisting.

Poolside in Dubai, we talked with a woman, Janet, who worked at the US embassy there. "I never want to leave here," she told us. "They're going to have to drag me out of here."

Her husband was a friend of mine. It was November, and the weather was gorgeous. Janet told us that her aunt had a bad reaction when she learned they were heading to the Middle East.

"Why are you taking my niece to Abu Ghraib?" she yelled at my friend.

"No, no," he told her. "Abu Dhabi."

"Abu Ghraib, Abu Dhabi—it's all the fucking same," Janet remembered her aunt saying.

At the pool, she took another sip of her wine and said, "If she could see me now."

We used to love flying into the airport there. The countries we were in have some strong points, but smell, generally speaking, is not one of them: festering garbage like meat gone bad; sweat; that dirty-dusty smell that gets into your clothes and bags; burning trash that must have included hair, Styrofoam, and motor oil, given the stench of it. Often, it felt as if we were sitting in a sauna—as if we couldn't quite pull enough oxygen into our lungs. But as soon as we got into the airport, it was as if the air had been purified and we could breathe again. My friend once took pictures of the bathroom.

"Man, I've never seen a bathroom as clean as this," he said.

That was our break from terrorism: Muslims, Christians, Jews, and undoubtedly atheists hanging out on the beach, happily and peacefully doing their own thing. Is there really a war between East and West, Islam and Christianity? Obviously, there are better ways to do things.

The Emirates have had some issues, like any other country.

But so do we.

TWENTY THE SETUP

IN JANUARY 2006, WE landed in an airfield in East Africa. We had fixers there who would meet us with SUVs and equipment. We were tracking al-Qaeda East Africa and al-Shabaab, which is affiliated with al-Qaeda East Africa.

My wife didn't know where I was, and that was, as usual, tough on her. So for this trip, she decided to take our daughter to Egypt to visit her parents. She had been working, earning her master's degree, and taking care of our daughter while I was gone. She definitely did not know what I was up to.

In Africa, a couple of thousand miles away from her, six of us emerged from a helicopter: two from my unit, two Navy SEALs, and two civilian guys from other agencies.

One of them was wearing sandals.

"Jack, you're seriously going to wear sandals into a shithole country?" we teased. "Sandals?"

"I'm just relaxed," he said.

"Dude, you need to wear shoes," I said.

"Why?" he said. "It's fucking hot."

"Because you can't run in sandals," I said.

"Run from what?" He seriously seemed to think he was on vacation.

We were supposed to land in the airfield and go directly into town. But our equipment in the field hadn't been serviced for a while.

"Let's just wait here while we take care of it," I said, "and then we'll move to our next location."

By the grace of God.

As we worked on the equipment, our fixers showed up and burst out of their vehicles.

"You guys need to leave now," they said. "Right now."

I'd never seen them look so nervous. Al-Shabaab—Aden Ayro's group—had set up an ambush and planned to attack us on our way into town. When we hadn't moved, they assumed we were going to stay at the airfield, so they had stormed a couple of checkpoints and were on their way to kill us.

Even as our guys told us the news, al-Shabaab barreled down dusty roads toward us, weapons bared in the back of white pickup trucks.

Our pilot spoke the local language, but he was about as calm as they come.

"You guys need to get on the aircraft right now," he said. "Right now."

We were within five minutes, tops, of being captured or killed—all of us.

Our commo guy was so unorganized. He kept dropping shit as he ran. Stop. Pick it up. Run. Stop. Pick it up. Run.

Sensitive items—they needed to make it to the bird.

Jack's sandals slowed him down.

"Move!" I yelled.

"Go! Go! Go!" the pilot yelled. We half handed, half dragged people into the aircraft.

"We're in," we all yelled at once.

He took off with the door still open and the tiny stairwell still down. We were still trying to get to our seats.

We were fucking terrified.

As we started to take off, we could see new pickups loaded with weapons heading toward us.

Me and the three other military guys pulled out broken-down M4 semiautomatic carbines and calmly put them back together. We were ready, but we didn't have enough ammo to take out the militia. And we could only do so much from the air. We absolutely would not risk another *Black Hawk Down*.

We didn't have to use them.

When we had reached a safe distance, the military guys calmly broke down their M4s and hid them.

"Hey, Jack," we said. "You never saw that."

"Got it," he said. "Glad you guys had it."

"And next time?" I asked.

"Right," he said. "Shoes."

We did not write about the M4s in the report. We maintained that we had only pistols because if the State Department had found out, it would have been an issue. But we weren't stupid.

The local guys who helped us remained on the airfield, and as we looked out, we watched their firefight, just as worried for them as we were for ourselves. We hoped they had enough firepower. We found out later that a couple of the guys had been killed. One lost an eye—we saw him about a week later, on another bad day. They had cleaned him up and then replaced his eye with a cow's eye.

I don't think anyone intentionally ratted us out that day. I think the locals grew complacent. They figured nothing would ever happen to us. So, when they knew we were coming, they'd throw a feast for us for lunch, and it didn't take a genius to figure out that when one of the guys went and bought all the food in the market, we were on our way.

And al-Shabaab probably saw the aircraft before we landed.

Later, we learned communications had been intercepted that said, "The white pigs have landed." In Islamic culture, pigs are considered impure. I might be impure, but if you're going to call me a pig, at least call me a brown pig.

I talked to the team about switching things up after that so we wouldn't be such obvious targets. We knew they were after us.

We arranged to meet the guys again to continue our work. We needed to keep looking for the terrorists who had received safe haven after the 1998 embassy bombings.

The airfield attack had been on a Saturday.

Later that week, a woman reached out to one of our linguists and asked if he would meet her for dinner because she said she needed some help. The woman knew the linguist's sister back home in the United States, who knew her brother worked at the embassy, but she didn't know what he did there.

In any case, our linguist met the woman for dinner on a Tuesday.

She allegedly told him her husband's bank accounts had been frozen. The woman gave him a phone number for her husband and said, "He'd like to talk with someone from the embassy."

But as she told her story, the linguist freaked out because he realized her husband was possibly involved in the same terrorist activities we were investigating. Our linguist was solid—great guy.

He was so upset about what she told him that he went straight from the dinner—to my house to tell me.

"Hey," I said, "were you followed?"

He didn't think he was.

Thursday morning, we went out on another mission. Because of the airfield incident, we changed the time, as well as a few other things, to make it less predictable. In and out.

That evening—or the next morning—we left for another mission at four o'clock. We got up at about one, and we hadn't slept all day because we had the earlier daytime mission. We completed the second mission, we came back, we cleaned our gear, and then we went back to our houses. My housemate was also my teammate from my unit. Hell of a guy. He and I relaxed for a bit and watched TV. Later that day, I went out on my own to get something to eat. My compound had maybe ten houses in it.

When I came back from dinner, our gate guard opened the

door for me to let me back in. Then I drove to my house. When I got out of my car, there were three guys behind me.

I heard a gunshot.

I realized I couldn't capture all of the men, but I grabbed one, and we fought for three or four minutes. Everything happened so fast, but even as we struggled, I wondered if they had followed the linguist the night he had dinner with the terrorist's wife.

Had it been a setup?

The other two guys grabbed at my arms and pulled the first guy free.

They ran. The gate guard was nowhere to be seen.

I stood alone in the cold, dark parking lot. I put my hand on my stomach.

It was wet.

Fucking brilliant, I thought. *I got shot.*

TWENTY-ONE   A LEAP OF FAITH

AT FIRST, I THOUGHT he had missed and it was just a rico-
chet. But when I felt the blood flooding my shirt, I knew I was in
trouble.

After my buddy opened the door to our house, I asked him to
call the team to warn everyone and to get me a fucking ambulance.
I was okay—I tried to reassure myself and my teammate. He called
the embassy. The embassy tried to call an ambulance, but it was
taking too long.

I kept thinking about my father. He had died while I was on
that deployment, and the team sent me back for the funeral. It
was too soon for any more losses in my family. My daughter was
three, and my wife still in her twenties—too young for widow-
hood. From a distance, she kept me alive.

If I die, she's gonna be pissed.

"Hey, do you have a car?" I asked one of the guards. He said yes. "Cool. You're taking me to the hospital."

I was talking. I was aware. I didn't feel much pain. Yet.

He loaded me into his pickup truck. But I swear that guy hit every single speed bump on the way to the hospital. The drive didn't take long, but it had been two hours since the bullet had worked its way through my guts.

At the hospital, I tried to open the door of my makeshift ambulance.

"Hey, man," I said. "Unlock the doors."

"They're not locked," he said.

I tried again.

The driver got out, came around, and opened the door from the outside—obviously, it wasn't locked. I had lost so much blood that I was too weak to open the truck door. I tried to remember my name and my Social Security number. Of course, the first question they asked was "Who shot you?" I told them it was a robbery attempt.

I got out of the truck, holding my stomach because my guts were coming out, and they brought out an aluminum emergency bed. It was way too high. It was too high for a tall person, let alone a five-foot-one person.

"How the fuck am I gonna get on top of this?" I asked. "You need to bring it down."

"It's broken," they said. The truck door was still open, so I climbed back in and jumped up on the bed from the inside of the pickup. So I'm fucking around trying to get out of the truck and then trying to jump up on this stretcher, and it's cold.

At least, everything seemed colder with less blood flowing through my body.

I didn't have high hopes for the hospital after that. Inside, I saw incompetency all around me.

These dudes are going to fucking kill me, I thought.

I asked an incredibly competent nurse with a British accent to look for an exit wound. She couldn't hear me, and I didn't have the strength to speak up. I pulled her toward me: "Do I have an exit wound?" She flipped me on my side. Hard, as you would a fish you were about to fillet. I could feel my strength seeping away.

"Yes. You have an exit wound."

"Imagine you're drawing a line between the entry wound and the exit wound," I said. "What do you think it hit?"

"Your kidney," she said. "Ninety-nine percent, your kidney."

Awesome. I have two of those.

I was still talking and still aware, and my vitals were almost normal, and I was watching because I didn't want them to kill me. The hospital looked like something out of the 1950s, smelled like Lysol, and featured new innovations like catheters sitting in dishes on the floor.

They're going to fucking kill me.

But the nurse took control.

"Guys!" she yelled. "We need blood over here!"

I was wearing jeans, and she didn't want to ruin the jeans by cutting them off. She tried to help me take them off, but I argued with her: "Just cut them off. My guts are coming out of a hole in my stomach."

"Sir, those are nice jeans," she said. "Those are expensive."
She refused to cut them.

Then they brought over an X-ray machine, and they wanted me to sit up while they did it.

"Can you do an X-ray while I'm lying down?" I asked.

"No," they said. "It's broken."

That's when I felt the first shock of pain, and it felt as if my intestines had shifted—just dropped down. It was extraordinarily painful.

The anesthesia doctor showed up and took immediate command. She took my vitals, asked for extra blood, and prepared to put me to sleep. I was chatting with her as if everything were fine. Pretending. I didn't want her to put me to sleep—I was afraid it would be the last time.

"Do you know what happened to you?" she finally asked, wondering if I was in so much shock that I didn't realize I was in danger.

She didn't think I would live. I may have been in shock, but I also knew I needed to stay alert and I needed to beat down my fear to make sure I lived through the hospital. I was terrified.

About halfway through this, my housemate showed up. I had trusted him with my life long before being shot. He had been covered in blood after tending to me at the house, so he changed before meeting me at the hospital. I believe he also brought the embassy doctor with him. They had planned to medevac me to South Africa, but the embassy doctor said he knew the right doctor for the situation.

The embassy doctor called in another doctor who was originally from Pakistan. He was one of those guys who exude confidence. Soft-spoken. Not bragging on his credentials. I trusted him the moment he walked in.

By that point, I was still trying to show that I was in control, but I was scared deep down. I knew I might not make it out. I thought about my wife and my daughter.

"Hey, relax," the doc said, grabbing my hand. "I know what's going on. We're going to open you up, and we're going to clean you up, and we're going to put you back together. You'll be fine."

But my next of kin needed to sign paperwork saying it was okay to do the operation. My buddy was standing there.

"Are you his next of kin?" they wanted to know. He started to demur.

"You can sign it," I said, and I smiled. "It's not like we have a choice."

For fuck's sake. But I think he was worried. He didn't want me to die—and he sure as hell didn't want to be responsible for signing any paperwork that led to my death.

I remember talking to the doctor as they wheeled me away.

"Am I going to see you again?" I asked. I needed to know if he thought I would live through the surgery.

"You're definitely going to see me again," he said.

They took me off to do the surgery, and just like on TV, the anesthesiologist had me count down from ten.

"Hey, we're taking him to the theater," I heard someone say.

And the last thing I heard: "What?" my buddy said. "What theater? Why are you taking him to a theater?"

It was just how the Brits say "operating room."

The operation took about five hours. I woke up in the ICU in a hospital in the middle of Africa. I still wasn't clear about whether

I was going to die, and I figured if I did die, I would have died for the right reason. But I felt bad about letting the guys down and leaving my family behind.

I didn't die.

They moved me from the ICU the next day, and then they planned to medevac me to Germany, but I was exhausted. The embassy doc told them to keep me at the hospital for two days.

So now I was in a hospital in the middle of Africa, and I really needed a bath.

"Sir, I have to give you a bath," a man named Patrick said with a thick African accent. He was my nurse for the weekend.

So that felt extremely awkward. I'm a Special Forces manly man, beefy shoulders and too much testosterone and all that, and this dude wants to give me a bath. This is not how Hemingway told it. The nurse was supposed to be gorgeous. And female. Definitely female.

But I needed a bath. So I let him.

He was a great guy, and I will be forever grateful to the medical staff at that hospital. They had limited resources, but they did everything they could to reassure me and keep me comfortable. Just like the strangers who helped me when I arrived in New York, these strangers didn't know anything about me. They were just good humans.

When I got shot, my buddy—for security, I will just refer to him as Mr. T—did not miss a beat. Mr. T had to take over as senior because I was of no use whatsoever, but he also came to the hospital every day. He signed the consent form, as my "next of kin," for them to perform the surgery. He reported what was going on and kept me in the loop. We moved houses for security—all of the houses. We didn't want them to find anyone else on the team. He packed my bag. He moved me from the hospital to the hotel to stay for about a month before they sent me back to the States.

When my guys moved me to the hotel, I opened my bag. Inside, I found the shirt I had been wearing when I was shot. It had a hole in it, but it was clean and folded neatly. My jeans had been washed and ironed like new. At the hospital, they had even washed the blood out of my shoes and cleaned and shined them.

Are these the clothes I was wearing? I thought. In the United States, they would have just cut them off me—and that would have been fine. I remembered my childhood with one pair of brown shoes. I had lived in the United States almost long enough to take a closetful of clothing for granted.

At the hotel, Mr. T brought me food every day and ate with me. I had trusted him with my life, and he came through. I forever owe him for what he did.

The Unit sent a doctor from back home. That doctor flew with narcotics, and I was going to need them. But the dude looked as if he was twenty, and I was pretty upset. I was stoned and wired, and I hadn't slept, and I couldn't believe they sent me Doogie fucking Howser to take care of my ass in a third-world country.

He gave me some pain pills.

"They already gave me pain pills at the hospital," I said, because I was being an ass.

"They gave you aspirin," he said. I'm sure he was used to dealing with the likes of me. "When was the last time you slept?"

I had to think about it.

It had been before I was shot—long before.

"Maybe two weeks?" I said.

He gave me some meds, and that was the first time I slept deeply in a long time.

I met him for breakfast the morning we were supposed to leave—I couldn't eat a lot because my intestines had recently had an out-of-body experience.

"I'm really sorry," I said, out loud, "but how old are you?"

He was nice about it.

"Listen," he said. "People think I'm a kid, but my son is in college. I've been practicing medicine for twenty years, and I know what I'm doing."

He was a lieutenant colonel.

We flew business class so we could stretch out. He was great—he kept checking in on me, giving me painkillers, and making sure I could sleep and was okay.

Doogie always comes through in the end.

The day after I got home, it snowed. My wife looked out the window, and two guys from the Unit—guys who were like brothers to me—played in front of my house as they shoveled snow and cleared off our cars.

We are like family.

In Washington, they offered me the option to continue my military career or potentially take a full early retirement. It could be enough for my family to live off—and included full benefits—and it would have provided me an opportunity to launch a second career while reaping the benefits of the first.

But while I was at Walter Reed's trauma center for a checkup, I watched the people around me. I saw a woman with one leg. I saw a guy, maybe twenty, with one arm and one leg, and he was learning to walk again. And there was me with both my kidneys—the bullet had missed—and half of my intestine. They brought the guy a boiled egg and a banana for breakfast, and I watched as his mom peeled them for him.

How do you peel a boiled egg or a banana with one hand?

I watched another guy as he learned to use his prosthetic hand. I just had so much respect for everyone there.

Through all of this, I had everything I could ever need. My team took care of my family, and they took care of me while I recovered. I'd had a pretty good career. I was mostly in one piece.

A beehive of nurses and doctors cared for these guys equally—officer, enlisted, Black, brown, white, and even the Arab they didn't know was an Arab. The level of support blew me away.

I'm not going to lie to you. I did think about leaving the military. But when I sat there looking at this kid with one hand calmly working to eat a banana, I thought, *You can't leave these guys.*

A nurse saw the guy's mom was near tears. "Trust me," she said. "Your son will be okay."

The doctor came to see me.

"You know what?" I said. "I'm fine."

"But you're not," he said.

"I am," I said. "I walked in here. I have both my legs. I shook your hand. I have both my eyes. I'm fine."

He tried to get me to sit so we could talk about it.

"These guys need you more," I said. And I left.

I had more fighting to do.

I RESTED FOR A bit, and then I deployed again.

Somewhere easy, they said.

Somewhere safe, they said.

I deployed as a basic communications guy. No heavy lifting. No shooting. No midnight raids.

I went to work in the morning, I did my thing, and I went home for the night. I worked at an embassy, and it was gorgeous. There was some crazy counterintelligence going on against everyone who worked at the embassy, so there was some nonsense: I'd go to my hotel and find that all of my clothes had been rifled through and thrown on the floor. I was pretty sure I hadn't left them there.

"Hey," I'd say, calling down to the front desk. "Any idea why my suitcase has been dumped on the floor?"

"No, sir."

"Somebody must have come to my room."

"I will investigate and let you know, sir."

"Somebody took my jacket."

"Gosh, nobody saw anyone in your room, sir."

There was the usual bullshit: on my first day, when I gave the Marine Corps gunny working the front gate my American diplomat passport, he asked if I had found it in the street.

"Man, check the picture," I said. "It's me."

He finally let me in.

Overall, though, it was a good gig. Good food. Interesting culture. Safe.

One morning, I walked to work just as I always did. I went through the front door, and then I hiked up to my floor. Just as I made it to the third-floor office—about a minute and a half later—I heard an explosion.

It sounded like a grenade.

The guy with me, a civil engineer, immediately dropped to his knees and pulled out his rosary. I realized he hadn't been trained to do anything different. In fact, he had been trained to do exactly what he did. Score one, Catholic Church.

"Please, God," he said, "make this a drill."

"Dude," I said. "Get up. It's not a drill. A grenade just exploded."

He wasn't my typical teammate—he was overweight, and, after he put away his rosary, his next instinct was to call his mother.

"If you do that, it will be your last fucking goodbye," I said, hoping my language would shock him into action. "But if you get your shit together, you can give her a call after we're out of this, and you can tell her you're safe—and maybe brag about your bravery."

I was calm, just as I had been trained to be. How could I defend the team? How could I calm the situation?

Of course, the painkillers still numbing my innards didn't hurt my sense of well-being. Mostly, though, my adrenaline kicked in, and I didn't feel any of my usual gut pain.

The explosion reminded me of the explosions I had heard during selection. And I was definitely not dead.

Sweet.

Next?

I locked the door—it was a vault door, like from a bank—to keep everyone inside safe.

We had a security destruction plan, which meant we had to destroy anything classified if it looked as if the embassy were going to be overrun—as in *Argo*. We got everything ready. My coworker needed something to do, so I had him call it in to headquarters that we might implement the destruction plan.

I also had the safe ready with our communications equipment so I could zero it out. Before we did that, I wanted to find the defense attaché, who is usually the most senior guy at the embassy, to get the go-ahead. And he may have had more information than my coworker and I did.

I found him low crawling under a desk.

"Sir, here's some body armor," I said. "Put it on, and let's go upstairs, and you can make the call back to headquarters in DC."

He made some calls, and we put the destruction plan on hold for a bit.

It just so happened that someone had mailed a shipment of

weapons, and they were in the mailroom. So that's what I needed to do next: I needed to open those boxes.

I didn't know if the terrorists had made it inside the embassy or if they would be waiting outside the vault after we unlocked the door. The Marines didn't know what was going on—nobody knew what was going on.

We heard another explosion. We had to get out of there.

But I had another fear: If the Marines who worked for the embassy saw a brown man in civilian clothes burst out of the vault with an M4 semiautomatic weapon, what would they do?

They would shoot.

If there were local terrorists outside the door, they would also shoot, because they would know I wasn't one of theirs.

We heard gunshots.

Man, this is bullshit! I came here to recover.

I had to get out. I opened the door, and I ducked low, and I ran.

I'm not going to fucking die here.

I made it to the first floor and ran toward one of the offices, looking for the other guy from my unit.

I didn't leave Africa to die in some damned glitzy embassy.

I heard a female voice.

"Were you shot?" she said.

What the fuck? The timing seems off for telling war stories, lady.

"Who's talking?" I asked. "Where are you?" And then I saw her hiding under a desk. She also had done what she was trained to do. I don't know who the fuck came up with the idea that hiding under a desk can protect you from explosions.

Shit, I thought, after her soft voice reminded me of home. *My wife's going to see this on the news. She doesn't even know where I am, but she'll know.*

She had been oddly upset when I hadn't immediately told her I got shot in Africa, and I did not need her to see "American soldier killed in random-ass bullshit at a random-ass embassy."

"Come with me," I told the woman. By then, we had a pretty raggedy crew, with my overweight coworker, the lady under the desk dressed for a day at the office, my military counterpart with his weapon, and one of the armed Marines we had encountered in the hallway. As long as I was with my white-guy counterpart, I had cover.

The two military guys and I rushed up to the roof with our M4s from the mail room.

Then the Marine looked at me as if something had suddenly dawned on him, and he asked, "How did you get such a high-speed weapon?"

I'm pretty sure he wasn't asking out of admiration.

"It's cool, man," my counterpart said. "We're both US Army Special Forces."

"Thank God," the Marine said. "Are you guys senior to me?"

"We are," my teammate said. You could see the relief on the guy's face—he was a young Marine, and it was probably obvious we were old enough to have some rank on him.

We looked over the wall. We could see what was going on on the ground, but they couldn't see us. The local guards for the embassy were holding their ground—and we could see no one had made it inside.

"Hey!" the Marine yelled. "I see somebody with a weapon!"

The Marines are very disciplined.

"Permission to fire, sir?" he asked.

"Man, don't fucking fire at anybody," said my counterpart, who was senior to me, as well. "That dude's security."

Brown guy. Local brown guy. Good guy.

"The terrorists are under us," I said.

There was nothing we could do from the roof as we listened to the battle rage below us. After a while, we heard another explosion—but this time, the jarring sounds of metal crashing and glass falling to the ground followed it.

A cloud of black smoke rose up from beneath us, and then we heard nothing.

The whole thing lasted about an hour, hour and a half.

And then I called my wife.

"Hey," I said. "You're going to see something on the news. But this is me talking to you, so you know I'm okay."

I didn't die.

The attack came from another Islamic extremist group.

When we watched the embassy video later, we realized just how close we had all come to a massacre. One minute and twenty-eight seconds after I went through the front door, the terrorists drove up. The guys in the car in front of the walk-in entrance jumped out and fired at everything moving.

They shot and killed a bystander walking past the door one minute and twenty-eight seconds after I had gone through it. If I had been a moment later . . .

Funny thing, in the not-ha-ha way, is that the terrorist appears to have had a moment of conscience. The embassy had two doors: one for people to walk through and one for people to drive through. The terrorists had two vehicles, one filled with propane tanks in front of the door people used to walk into the building. I think that one was meant as a distraction. The second one was meant to drive through the motor-pool doors. That second vehicle—it was a small pickup truck—would have to slam the metal motor-pool doors to make it through. On either side of the doors stood big decorative pillars. And just as the driver of the pickup truck got ready to slam the doors, an older lady started to cross the street in front of him.

The terrorist, who was on a mission to kill a bunch of innocent people at an embassy, didn't want to hit an old lady, so he slammed into one of the pillars rather than the metal doors.

But it was only momentary. He got out of the truck, and he had a detonator in his hand. He ran to the other vehicle—the one with the propane tanks—and he grabbed an AK-47 and started firing from behind the car.

The neighborhood had five or six embassies close to one another, and the Chinese embassy sat closest to ours. One of their guys went to a window to see what was happening and got shot in the neck. The terrorists weren't targeting anyone—they were just shooting.

The guy in the window died.

The local guys who pulled security for our embassy reacted fast—we weren't in a country that is necessarily friendly to the United States, but those guys did their jobs well and properly protected diplomatic missions on their soil. Local security killed the four terrorists and then hit the propane tanks in the car. When the car exploded, it ensured the terrorists had breathed their last.

Afterward, the Marine offered his commendations.

"You guys did really well today," he said.

"Thanks, man," I said. "Do you remember when you asked me if I had found my US passport in the street?"

His face fell.

"I'm really sorry," he said.

I think he was. And maybe he didn't make assumptions about the next brown guy he saw.

That evening, the adrenaline disappeared. I felt drained. My body was still recovering from my injuries, and I was just done in a way I hadn't been on previous missions.

The next day, I walked to the office.

"Man, you're bad luck," the guys from the Unit teased. "Even when we send you to the nice places, all hell breaks loose."

TWENTY-THREE

JACKPOT.

After the missiles had been launched by the Navy ships sitting off the Horn of Africa and as we waited for confirmation, I thought about the mission.

Aden Ayro.

There's no way he could have escaped again, I thought. *Right?*

Ayro and his ilk were affiliated with both the guys who shot me and the guys who had bombed the embassies.

Jackpot.

The missiles had launched, and Eddie and I had headed home. We knew they had hit their target, but we didn't know if Ayro had been killed. I needed confirmation. And a nap. I felt like shit.

A year after the embassy incident, I had deployed back to Africa to go after the leader of Hizbul Shabaab in Somalia. My guts had, for the most part, healed, and I was ready.

But hours before the final mission to go after him, I started coughing. Violently. I wasn't even sick—I'm just allergic to dust or Somalia or something.

"Hey, man, this is really bad," I said to our team medic. He'd been hitting me with every kind of drug to try to get rid of it. He knew that I had to go back out that evening—that I had to get Ayro.

"Maybe you should rest?" he said. But I knew we were close. So close. I still had plans to make and things to double-check.

The medic hit me with a cortisone shot. It worked.

My body had been through a lot. My stomach didn't process well on a good day, and Africa was rarely a good day. To get information, we had to get friendly with the locals—and that always meant food. Even if the food was good, the aftermath usually wasn't.

The food wasn't good. When we wanted something to eat, we went to a restaurant that was basically a shack made of tent canvas. They brought us fish straight from the ocean, fried in a frying pan. Guts and all.

With our contacts on the ground, we often ate something called tuna loaf—basically a mound of tuna with tons of fucking mayonnaise on it. You look at it, and you just can't. But we did. Mission first. They also brought us camel milk. It was warm and salty and tasted a bit like something that had been burned. In a lawn mower. It wasn't good.

After eating the tuna and the mayonnaise and the smoky, salty camel milk, we got into our shitty SUVs. The locals drove crap cars. They imported used vehicles from everywhere, so some of the cars had the steering wheels on the left, and some had the steering wheels on the right. There were no paved roads. There were no traffic lights. No signs.

Our contacts on the ground made sure our SUVs were outfitted with AK-47s. Usually, we rode in the back. In the back-back, without any seats. The daily temperature in May was about 89 degrees, so not yet miserable but not exactly comfortable when crammed in the back-back with another dude. Another big dude.

Tuna loaf. Mayonnaise.

We put up with all the suck for a bigger cause: a safer America. For me, each of my actions demonstrated to my team, to my organization, and to the US Army how immigrants can further the cause. Together, we are stronger. In Africa, where I'm from, they say, "You can go fast alone but go far together."

In the United States, where I'm also from, they say, "Immigrants—we get the job done."

At any moment, if I wished to no longer be in the Unit, I could ask to be reassigned—no questions asked. It was stressful. It was difficult being away all the time. It was hard to keep my head straight when I had several different personas. It sucked to be shot.

But I had more work to do.

Before each of our big missions, McChrystal, even as a task force commander, would visit us—unless he couldn't get in for security reasons. It was like getting a visit from the tooth fairy before you lost your tooth. I don't know when that guy slept, but it was great because he'd always say, "We've got your back."

Except on that mission. He had no troops available for a quick reaction force. No one would be able to help for at least twelve hours.

"If anything happens to you guys," he told us, "you're on your own."

Hoo-ah, sir.

But we'd made it out safely. Had Ayro?

Eddie and I went to the dining facility, starving, at our small base in Africa to get some breakfast after the missiles hit their marks. As usual, we were silent professionals. As we ate our eggs, CNN came on and announced that there had been an air strike that had killed Aden Ayro. All around us, we could hear soldiers talking about it.

"I'll bet we did it."

"I don't think it was us."

"I'll bet it was the French."

They had no idea.

Then I heard a soldier say, "We should kill all of 'em. Blast those countries to glass. We should kill every fucking Muslim on this planet."

He was a young guy, and I'm sure he didn't mean anything by it—just talking the shit he'd been taught to talk—but I couldn't help thinking, *You're proud of this hit. You're proud of me.*

I was sitting right behind him—I could see who said it—but I couldn't say anything. I couldn't say, "No. You need the fucking crazy-determined Muslim Egyptian with the hole in his stomach."

I wanted to tell him we had a lot more in common than we had differences.

An al-Shabaab spokesperson did me the biggest favor of my life: he went on BBC and confirmed Ayro's death. We got the right guy. We learned two others connected with the embassy bombings had also been killed that day. Nobody knew we were involved. I can't tell you the satisfaction that comes from doing a job simply because it needs to be done, rather than for any kind of bragging rights.

Exhausted, I went to sleep.

The next day, we learned that when we hit Ayro, we hit another high-ranking al-Qaeda guy, as well as seven other people, including Ayro's wife—who was the only person believed to be innocent. I wondered why she had stayed with a man like that. Could she have left? Had she chosen him? Everybody else provided security or was part of al-Shabaab—all bad. And each of their bodies burned.

The spokesperson for al-Qaeda East Africa vowed retaliation. He said he would kill all of us. But in one of his statements, he said that Ayro's wife's body was intact. It didn't burn.

That's God's punishment, I thought. *God wanted them to burn.*

But she was innocent. I thought that was also God.

For three days, we didn't move from the base. We didn't make any movement at all—we didn't want anyone to associate us with what had just happened. Then we went back to the task force. Everyone was celebrating Cinco de Mayo and the success of the mission.

They put us in for medals for that, but everything we did went through the task force in Iraq. We were not on the priority list, and the task force there didn't seem to have a grasp of anything that was going on outside Iraq. They were all wrapped around the axle on their own mission, which is a good thing. We never got any medals for that mission. Ultimately, it didn't matter: it's not like anybody cares how many awards you have after you leave the military. And we knew what we'd done.

To me, my Purple Heart was much more important, but not because I needed an award for some asshat shooting me in the guts. It's not an award. It's a benefit. It meant there were places in the United States where I or my children could get a free university education. That's everything. That's the future.

Eddie was also a Purple Heart recipient, but to his credit, he has kept fighting for the award from his mission in Africa. I hope he gets it.

After Ayro's death, the work didn't end, of course. We continued tracking the smuggling routes.

I worked with a great woman operative on a mission. GPS was a shit show then, as I mentioned when I talked about the illegal gun market. She and I were driving to find a specific bad guy's house, and Garmin still needed some expertise in that country—it just wasn't accurate. Garmin showed us driving straight into the house we were looking for. That didn't make sense. We were in the middle of fucking nowhere, in another little area where everybody knew everybody. We planned to just drive by the house—to get eyes on and see what we could see.

We hit a dead end. Right in front of the bad guy's house. Across the street, there was another house, and the owner stood outside.

"What are you guys doing?" he asked, in Arabic. "This is a dead end."

No shit.

"I didn't know," I said.

"Everybody knows that," he said.

"I'm not from here," I said. "I'm lost."

No shit.

But the operative gave me cover because obviously, I wouldn't be doing anything shady if I had a woman with me. Culturally, if they wanted to believe women are incapable of being badasses, I'm totally cool with using that to my advantage. He didn't see her as a threat.

But because she was a badass, her training kicked in immediately.

We had to use the guy's driveway to make a U-turn. I had equipment in my backpack, and she had a weapon in hers.

"Hey, what happened to Arabic hospitality?" I asked. "You're not even going to invite us in for a cup of tea?"

Balls before brains, man. Ovaries, too.

"You know what?" the guy said. "I will invite you. Come inside."

I rolled up my window and turned to my companion. "You're my Russian bride," I said. "You don't speak Arabic or English." We happened to be in an Arabic-speaking country, and many foreigners there married Russian women.

"Got it," she said. She was switched on. I turned on the communication system in my backpack just in case he or his pals kidnapped or killed us.

We went inside the house across the street from the bad guy, and we had a cup of tea. He brought us food, and we chatted.

I engaged in conversation, but I also thought about what I would do if my communication system made a noise, which it sometimes did. And I tried to think about what I would do if it melted down and started to smoke, which it also sometimes did. How would I make it look normal? We always had a story.

Here's the thing: If you think you have a booger hanging out of your nose and you keep checking for it, then everyone's going to notice. You have to pretend that everything's normal.

We stayed inside the house for an hour and a half.

It didn't scare us until afterward, but until that point, it was pure training.

And drive.

For me, this was a war that could not be lost. After I was shot, there was no "Hey. I'm tired. Someone else will take over." I understood that I had something the other guys didn't have. I also wanted to defend my new way of life—my American way of life—as well as my Muslim way of life, which is also very much American and very much unseen.

As part of my Muslim way of life, I knew that I had helped a lot of locals, too, by avoiding misunderstandings, misinterpretations, and intentional misreadings. If we did our jobs right, innocent people would not be killed.

That's what kept me going. It was a lot bigger than just me.

And in the continual game of Whac-A-Mole, Ayro's replacement had already popped up.

SALEH ALI SALEH NABHAN.

You get one militant, and another one pops up. That's why we wanted to keep getting at the source, keep hitting it hard in Africa. In addition to replacing Ayro, Nabhan had been involved with multiple attacks in Kenya in 2002, as well as the 1998 embassy bombings, so he was on the FBI's most-wanted list.

He had already been in place before we got Ayro, and in some ways, he was higher up the chain, but it's more like one guy was the CEO and the other was the COO. Ayro was a major player and had been running the show. Nabhan was mostly just harder to catch than Ayro.

Nabhan disappeared because he knew we wanted him.

He didn't stay anywhere long, so if we were going to get him, it had to be while he was traveling. But we didn't want to hurt anyone he was traveling with or near. We started looking at POL—pattern of life. If he prayed five times a day, it set a pattern. But we didn't know, from moment to moment, where he was. If a source gave us good information, he might just as suddenly say, "Nope. Moved. We don't know where he is."

But people talk.

"Did you see Nabhan's new baby/chicken/AK-47?"

Sit at a café and listen. Ask somebody in a village in Africa about their childhood, and that person will tell you everything. Just like the States. And we worked in areas that didn't focus on individualism: Communities did things together. If someone was sick, the whole village knew. Funeral? Everybody went. It was a social obligation. And one piece of information led to another piece.

As usual, we operated out of a neighboring country. We had equipment set up in different places to track him. At that point, more than a hundred people made up the task force: we had Navy SEALs, a few Unit guys, people from the FBI, people from other government organizations. Every morning, at nine o'clock, we'd talk: "Okay, what do you have?" The collaboration was phenomenal because everybody put their bit of information on the table. Everybody had a piece of the puzzle, but nobody had the whole puzzle.

The collaboration also allowed us to sniff out bad information from a source who hoped to mislead us.

The terrorists could be clever.

"Hey, can you bring me Monica?" we heard.

Who the fuck is Monica? And that doesn't sound like an Arabic name. We thought they were talking about a woman, but they were talking about vehicles. In this case, they named an SUV after Monica Lewinsky because she had a "big butt." "Hey, did you see Monica yesterday?" We honestly thought they had kidnapped a westerner named Monica. Another time, they named a car after an Egyptian actress because the car had big headlights.

We finally figured it out while I was chatting with our house guard.

"Did you see the new Monica so-and-so bought?" he said.

They had codenames for everything, and he told me what they were—it was common in that town. At first, the terrorists used these codenames, and then everybody started using them.

It took a year, but we got Nabhan through his wife: everybody has an anchor—even terrorists. Everyone assumes the women aren't important enough to be watched, so the women continue on with their shopping and visiting. It wasn't easy for them to move far because they had kids or guards.

Nabhan and his wife did not live physically near each other. But he sent messages: Give her my new phone number. Tell her where I am.

People talk. Just be patient.

Nabhan always stayed in populated, congested areas, which made it difficult to, say, hit his house with a missile or three. We knew he had to perform his midday prayer, so we started doing the math on traffic patterns. If he left here at this time, he'd arrive here at this time.

We thought about options.

During Ramadan, Nabhan would break the fast with his family. The good thing about Ramadan is that everything becomes regimented: I looked up prayer times on the internet, and boom. Golden. But we didn't want to kill a guy breaking the fast with his family. In fact, we had serious debates about whether we should target anyone during Ramadan, but my feeling was that if he was a bad guy, he was a bad guy during Ramadan, too.

One of our guys thought maybe he could hide in a trunk all day, spring out, and—too hot in Mogadishu in September to put a guy in a trunk. Also, he looked like a white guy from the Midwest, being that he was a white guy from the Midwest, and there was no way he'd escape.

We would bring in the big guns.

As Nabhan drove a pickup truck down the highway just south of Mogadishu to meet his wife, three Little Birds appeared from nowhere (but really from a ship off the coast of Somalia). Bam! Bam! And they shot him and the guy with him in the truck.

People pulled off the highway to watch. The helicopters landed. Navy SEALs emerged, grabbed the body, gathered any intel from the truck, and disappeared. They were in and out in five minutes. Just gone.

It was like something out of a movie. Eyes on, take off, done.

Then we saw it on the news: they said it was the French because they were wearing French uniforms. They were not. They were wearing American uniforms. The US government made an announcement that it was the SEALs.

Nabhan was the first guy buried at sea. There is a process for Muslims who die at sea. In Nabhan's case, that's not exactly what happened. But they weren't going to leave the guy in the street— they had to take the body to identify it, and they wanted to check for intelligence, such as his phone or other information he might have had with him. The Navy flew in a Muslim chaplain.

Burying him at sea meant there would be no eternal wailing over the grave of a false martyr. It laid the groundwork for bin Laden's burial.

ON ONE OF MY last missions, we worked with another country's special operations units. The head of their intelligence
service met with us. It was me, a Navy SEAL, a Marine, and a
government guy.

A guy from the host nation introduced everybody, but when he
got to me, the head of security services stared hard.

Did he recognize me?

"Are you with us or with them?" he asked the host-nation guy
in Arabic—assuming I didn't speak it. He wanted to know my
name.

He squinted at me. I looked like someone he knew from another country, he said, in Arabic.

Shit. Does the guy know me from somewhere else?

It was complicated to remember to keep things straight between deployments, work, and home life.

If he had asked me where I lived, I could have laid out my fake neighborhood. My street. The restaurants I liked to go to. How long traffic took from point A to point B.

"It always takes about a month before it feels as if you're normal," my wife said each time I returned home. She didn't understand why. I couldn't explain it to her. In her mind, I may have been from any other elite military unit, but I was always myself. She wouldn't have guessed my true mission.

The security guy looked as if he was trying to work a puzzle.

"No," another of the local guys said. "He's American military."

I held my breath.

"Well, he looks like us," the intelligence guy said. "I would have sworn you're an Arab."

In Arabic, I said, "You know what? I am."

And I told an off-color joke. Testosterone humor is the same everywhere.

The security guy laughed.

Then the security guy told a joke, in Arabic.

Safe.

We finished the meeting, and the local guys wanted to do some target training from a helicopter. I told them we wouldn't release weapons to them unless they showed us they knew how to use them. Early the next morning, we went to a training compound that had some old small weapons and some old small buildings. We gave them the coordinates for one of the small buildings.

"If you can hit this building from the helicopter, then we know you can use the weapons," we told them.

The buildings were in a big field about two miles long, and there was a guy standing on the side. There was an observation post where we could see the whole field with all these buildings their Special Forces guys used for training. The night before, they had argued for use of our radios so they could communicate with us, and they weren't super happy when we told them we weren't authorized to give them one of our radios.

Out on the field, this guy flew in with a Russian helicopter. We were up in the observation tower. Their guy gave him the grid coordinates. The pilot decided to fly in a certain direction and hit the target.

"Hey, man," I said to one of their guys. "If he does that, he's going to be facing us when he starts shooting."

"It's okay," he said. "He's the best pilot we have. He'll shoot down."

"Are you sure?"

"Yeah, yeah."

The pilot came in. He turned left, he turned right, he zigzagged toward the building, he flipped around, and he started firing as he was coming in low and fast.

Fine.

As he lifted the aircraft back up, he kept his finger on the trigger and fired just over our heads.

Thank God I'm short—it was that close. The Marine ran and hid behind the bleachers as if they'd stop bullets. The SEAL was videotaping it, so he didn't move because he didn't want to mess up the video. I don't know if that was brave or stupid.

I talked to the local guy.

"Hey," I said. "That was messed up. We could have been killed."

"No way, man," he said. "He's our best pilot."

He communicated with the pilot.

"Yesterday you guys were all concerned about radios," I said. "How are you talking to the pilot?"

"I'm calling him on his phone," he said.

"Right," I said, taking a deep breath. "So how did he get the grid coordinates?"

"Oh, he has a Garmin," the guy said.

So.

He was talking on his cell phone, holding his Garmin, flying a helicopter, and firing at the same time.

"Yeah," he said. "But don't worry about it. He's the best pilot we have."

"What did he tell you?" I asked.

"He's gonna try again," he said. "The sun was in his eyes."

Dude turned around. He came back. He went in for about two or three seconds, and then he lifted back up.

"Hey," I said. "What's up?"

"Oh, he was facing the mountain," he said.

"I think we should call it off," I said.

"No," he said. "One more time."

The third time he almost crashed.

That guy hit everything on that field except for the building.

"I don't think you guys are ready," I said. "I would hate to see your worst pilot."

We trained them some more, but we ended up leaving. Those guys were all about taking money and equipment from the

United States—they weren't terribly worried about catching terrorists. It's extremely unusual for our guys to work with other countries' militaries. I only did it that once.

After Nabhan, I spent some time in North Africa and then again in West Africa. I continued to track the flood of guys going to Iraq and Afghanistan, coming from Algeria, Niger, Libya, Morocco, and Mali.

During that time, one of my heroes, General Stanley McChrystal, got caught up in a scandal when a disingenuous, at best, *Rolling Stone* freelancer quoted remarks McChrystal's team had made about Vice President Joe Biden after a few drinks at a bar. The comments were disrespectful, and when President Barack Obama summoned McChrystal—commander of forces in Afghanistan at the time—McChrystal offered his resignation.

I didn't like how he left—how all that went down. But he left with such pride and dignity. He acknowledged his mistake, and then he stepped down with no drama. His retirement speech was a lesson in graciousness—and he later said he would vote for Biden for president.

The mission he built continued. We started tracking Boko Haram—they popped up in Nigeria and the surrounding countries after being founded in 2002. They've been aligned with the Islamic State of Iraq and the Levant since 2015, and they've killed tens of thousands of people. You might recognize them from when they abducted two hundred schoolgirls in 2014.

They are closely affiliated with the Muslim Brotherhood; their founder, Mohammed Yusuf, joined the Muslim Brotherhood when it moved to Nigeria.

During one of those missions, there was a threat to one of our embassies from al-Qaeda West Africa.

As has always happened throughout my career, they sent me in when the people on the ground didn't want us there. The woman who was in charge of security at the embassy took one look at me and decided I was a meathead. On some level, I enjoyed that. I was still short, but no one would have accused me of being scrawny.

We installed a bunch of surveillance equipment so people would be safe. I noticed there was a mosque right across from the embassy that didn't seem right. It had been built by the Libyans. I tried to explain to the regional security officer that something was up. She obviously hated her life and everybody else's life, but that wasn't my concern: I just wanted to keep people safe.

"I really think something's going on in the mosque," I said. There should have been people going in and out five times a day for prayers. I never saw anybody.

"You fucking military guys," she said. "You're just so fucking sensitive about mosques. You guys have this complex."

Because we're anti-Muslim, apparently.

I couldn't tell her. And she, apparently, thought I was a Mexican.

She said there were a lot of mosques in the city and people could go anywhere. But that's not how it works.

"That mosque is just weird," I told her, and we went back and forth about it. She wouldn't listen; I was a racist. Yada yada.

I told some other government guys, but then I left. Yes, there's some irony in that being my final experience while I was deployed. I guess I should be glad this lady was sticking up for all Muslims?

It wasn't the first mission where I encountered people who did not want me—the military guy—there because of assumptions about how we operate and how we think. I was often the only person on a mission, and my directive included this: "Some embassies are not military-friendly. The country is not American-friendly." I've gone in places where I worked with a US government civilian who said, "I don't like military guys. For damn sure, I don't like special operations guys. You have thirty days to prove to me why you should be here." A couple of times, after thirty days, they requested two or three more guys like me. Minority guys? Women? White operatives who could blend? We all could keep a low profile to get the job done. And we, the minority operatives in particular, were all used to coming up with alternative solutions to other people's bullshit—after swallowing down what we'd love to say and working to make them feel better about themselves. We'd been training our whole lives to implement change management. When the Unit needed someone to handle a sensitive situation, they sent me, the triple minority. However, after getting shot, I kept getting sick. One morning, I felt extreme pain in my stomach. I had eaten something in the hotel that just destroyed me. (Side note: One morning, I went for breakfast, and the president of Iran, Mahmoud Ahmadinejad, was sitting in the same restaurant. *If only he knew what an incredible target he is right now*, I thought. But that's not how we operate.)

My stomach was so bad that day that they sent me home. All the way home. I was, as always, part of that decision, and I worried that my constant stomach issues would put a mission at risk.

It was a long-ass flight.

When I got home, the Unit sent me straight to the doctor, where they discovered I had a parasite that needed to be wiped out. After all the places I've been, I'm sure there's still a parasite party going on in there. I'm sure some of my teammates have similar issues.

After that, my fourteenth deployment, I decided it was time to take a break. I wanted to spend more time with my family. My father had died just before I was shot, and my daughters were growing older. I went to another unit as a sergeant major, and, until I retired, I taught people everything I knew.

I've just spent many pages describing to you the bravery, intelligence, and strength—mental and physical—of the men and women in the Unit. But it's important for me to say this for the people I served with: war broke us down, too.

My body hurts, as do the bodies of many other veterans. We train hard, we carry heavy gear, and we jump out of vehicles and airplanes carrying all of our equipment. We twist ankles and backs, we fall, and we suffer gunshot and shrapnel wounds. I know this is the same for the grunts, medics, helicopter pilots, truck drivers, and cooks, too.

Sometimes, our minds also hurt.

I've been trained to deal with it, but just like being trained to deal with physical pain, that's part of the problem: Almost none of us know when to ask for help. I'm supposed to know how to deal with this shit on my own.

Many military units condition you not to ask for help; we are weak if we say we are tired, sick, or unable to sleep. Soldiers with security clearance worried they might lose their clearances if they sought mental health support. I hope that's not the case now.

I feel compelled to highlight those pains. It's okay to be sick, and it's okay to seek help. General Carter Ham set a profound example when he said he sought help for posttraumatic stress disorder when he was a two-star general. He wanted to set the example—I am sure it was not easy.

I have asked for help, and most people around me think I am doing pretty well, but that's my point: It's okay to ask for help, and we must encourage one another to seek help when needed. We must check on one another. We get used to checking on one another while serving, but once we are out, many of us feel alone. We lost operatives in our community to suicide, and it's not because they lacked strength and "intestinal fortitude."

I read an article recently about something called "operator syndrome"—or "allostatic load."[19] That's simply the stress both your body and your mind take over the years in the Special Forces. It comes from the same stuff everyone else in the military deals with: being away from home, watching people die, killing people, not getting enough sleep, being under constant stress, eating bad or insufficient food.

Tuna loaf.

It leads to much of what we've seen the "regular" men and women go through, too: We can't sleep. We have sleep apnea even though we're fit. Our heads hurt. We get depressed. We worry about stupid things. We sit facing the door. We have a hard time focusing.

Recovery for operatives is the same as for anyone else: talk to someone, keep working out, maintain a healthy diet, and get some damned sleep.

One thing is different for operatives, though. Try going to

19 Stew Smith, "Operator Syndrome: Managing High Allostatic Load," Military.com, https://www.military.com/military-fitness/operator-syndrome-managing-high-allostatic-load.

Veterans Affairs and asking for help when your record has been sanitized. I'm not going to go into deep detail about my interactions with VA here—everyone has a VA story—but I will say I've spent too much time trying to "prove" that I've been in the suck and that I've seen some stuff.

I do have a recommendation: I think it would be great if VA had one person with the clearance to deal with all of us so we wouldn't end up trying to convince some random human that we're not making up injuries to fraudulently claim benefits.

In any case, the mental and physical toll of deploying is real, so get help.

But even as my body started to break down and I wanted to spend time with my girls, I felt so guilty leaving. I felt as if I were leaving my guys behind. In some ways, that was great. Guys who didn't necessarily like me at first now said things like, "Man, you can't leave us. How are we going to do this without you?"

It was extremely hard for me.

When I told my boss, I just cried. These guys are my family.

"You have to take care of yourself and your wife and daughters, and we will keep going," he reassured me. "Everything will be fine."

I was home in time for the Fourth of July. It seemed fitting.

Soon after, in January, as I watched TV, President Obama announced that bin Laden had been killed.

You know what? I thought. *I think I'm fine. These guys are doing great.*

TWENTY-SIX   A PATH FORWARD

ON ONE OF MY deployments, we could see Kilimanjaro, the highest mountain in Africa. It rises up above the fig trees and the umbrella trees and the thornbushes—and giraffes and elephants—an unreal burst above the African plains. When the volcano erupted a million years ago, it left a dip at the top that gathers snow.

It seemed unreachable.

Of course I decided to climb it.

Maybe on the way out of this deployment?

But the military, after sending me to every shithole in the world, of course wouldn't let me climb a mountain on the way home from deployment because I might hurt myself.

I told the guys that as soon as I left the Unit, I would climb that mountain.

I had everything planned—I would go in January. I needed to challenge myself. I was forty-one and still constantly needed to prove myself. I would carry my American flag. I trained hard for it. A week before I was supposed to go, a family member with two young daughters died in a car accident. I postponed the trip.

But those daughters. I would use the trip to raise money for their education. As I was doing that, I was also thinking of my own daughters. What would happen if I didn't return from one of my deployments? Who would take care of them? I knew the Army would do a good job of making sure they got all their entitlements, but what was beyond that? Military families have much on the line, which many Americans do not realize. When soldiers die, they leave families behind who need more than financial support. They need to be loved, be parented, and have a family. I always kept that and my wife and daughters in mind while on missions. When a grenade landed feet away from me, I had my young daughter's contagious smile in mind. When I was in the hospital recovering from my gunshot wound, I had my older daughter's sense of humor putting a smile on my face. Family is what keeps you going. You live, maybe die, for it.

I climbed in June. Tanzania itself was warm, but in the arctic zone of the mountain—extreme altitude—the temperatures would drop far below freezing. My face would turn blue as I attempted the climb.

The guide sized me up. It didn't take long.

"Have you ever done anything like this before?" he asked.

"No."

He saw a short man who had never climbed before and undoubtedly made many assumptions. On the third day of the climb, he grew concerned.

"Hey," he said, "you need to slow down. You're moving really fast."

I got to the base camp ahead of everyone, so I went ahead and set up a tent. Two or three hours later, everyone else started to arrive. That meant that I had more time to rest than everybody else. The night of the summit, everyone typically begins the climb at around midnight so they arrive at the top at sunrise. If climbers arrive too early, it's too dark to see anything, and it's too cold to stick around. As soon as you stop, your body believes it's done and begins to shut down. That's when you feel the lack of oxygen and the cold.

I ran out of breath so quickly up there that in the morning, I put on one boot and then rested before I put on the other boot.

I told the guide I would like to start later than everybody else so I wouldn't reach the summit too soon. He argued with me. He worried that, because it was so dark, I would hurt myself and not have anyone to help.

That's reasonable.

Once again, in Africa, I was at the mouth of the river, thinking about solutions downstream. As I write this, the Muslim Brotherhood still occupies my mind—as does the solution to the equation: education. I believe that so thoroughly that I continue to monitor the four girls, now women, whose education I financed back home in Egypt. I wanted them to have an opportunity. I know that when the women of a household are educated, it changes the prospects for the whole family.

They're doing beautifully. One of them has the highest GPA in the city. But I'm a drop in the bucket.

I think about how much money we spend in Egypt reinforcing war—an allegiance based on the premise of continued war and an allegiance that, when the Muslim Brotherhood won political control of the country (which they've since lost), placed the money for weaponry directly into the hands of an organization that spawned every terrorist organization I and every other service member has battled in the past twenty years.

We spend $1.3 billion a year. I mean, we're basically paying them enough to create an arms race that's competitive enough to keep Israel and Egypt from killing each other. Who came up with that? Raytheon? That's how much we hand Egypt, with the assumption that they'll buy weapons from us—which makes it a nice little benefit for the American companies that produce the weapons of war.[20] Except that from 2015 to 2020, Egypt spent only 15 percent of that money on US products, down from almost 50 percent in previous years, and instead bought from France—and Russia.[21]

Not every guy in the Muslim Brotherhood is a bad person, and I think that if you can educate people, you can kill the "need" for terrorism—and for $1.3 billion worth of weapons.

Education.

Education is the only way not to leave a void when the American troops leave. Of course, a country's leadership often doesn't

20 Jeremy M. Sharp, "Recent Action on U.S. Foreign Aid to Egypt," *Egypt: Background and U.S. Relations*, Congressional Research Service, updated May 27, 2020, https://crsreports.congress.gov/product/pdf/RL/RL33003/112#page=28.
21 Bradley Bowman, Jared Thompson, and Ryan Brobst, "Egypt's Transition Away from American Weapons Is a National Security Issue," *Defense News*, May 25, 2021, https://www.defensenews.com/opinion/commentary/2021/05/25/egypts-transition-away-from-american-weapons-is-a-national-security-issue/.

want us to educate its people, because then the dynamic changes: educated people want better leadership.

If we don't educate them, somebody else will fill that void: ISIS. Russia. China. The Taliban. The Muslim Brotherhood. Where we see hopelessness, they see opportunity. They go in and take resources while providing basics—food, jobs, hope (even if it's false hope, hope is hope when you can't feed your family)—and then we act surprised when a modern version of colonialization happens and our enemies grow stronger.

I saw it first in Bosnia. In a struggling, war-torn population, Saudi Arabian extremists saw an opportunity to move from Islam light to Islam hate. In Bosnia, we—Americans—could have filled the void with something more secular, something aimed at engineering and technology and reconstruction and strong women and families.

We seem to believe we have two options: wage war or leave. There's a third option: level the field—provide opportunity so desperation doesn't create more hatred. Even now, we see the Qataris and Turks moving into Somalia; they see an opportunity for proxy war against other countries in the region. In the process, Somalia has become less stable and has lost traditional allies—including, ironically, Egypt. Turkey has also built its relationship with Somalia in recent years.

The guy who made the Muslim Brotherhood tapes in Alexandria when I was a kid? Wagdy Abd el-Hamied Mohamed Ghoneim? He's now based in Turkey, writing books and creating animated shows. He has a Facebook page, a Twitter feed, and a YouTube channel. In 2017, he was sentenced to death in Cairo, in absentia, for creating a terrorist group. But in May 2021, he led chants at the Israeli Consulate in Istanbul that recalled an ancient battle, Khaybar, where Muslims overcame Jews.

In other words, he's still out in the world, educating the masses, while we provide weapons.

We need a level policy. We need leadership that understands the culture or surrounds itself with people who do. We keep going back and forth. There are people in our government who think of the Muslim Brotherhood as allies.

No.

They hate us. Every radical Islamic group in the last hundred years has had affiliations with the Muslim Brotherhood. They start there; the Brotherhood recruits people in elementary school. And then the Brotherhood members get worse and become al-Jama'a al Islamis. Then they become worse, and they're al-Qaeda. And then they go up a level, and they're ISIS.

They're al-Shabaab in Somalia.

They issued fatwas against presidents in Egypt and US troops in Iraq.

Is the Muslim Brotherhood a big political party in the Middle East? Yes. I've seen people who think the Muslim Brotherhood is the best thing since Otto Rohwedder invented sliced bread in 1928 (oddly enough, the same year the Muslim Brotherhood was invented) because they've presented themselves that way—as a legitimate front for a political group.

Are they the route to democracy rather than authoritarianism? Are they better than authoritarianism? No. They are just another form of it—except, as their ideas trickle down to thugs seeking to prove themselves in destitute countries, the quest to create an Islamic state becomes more and more violent: beheading American journalists, hanging "infidels" in soccer stadiums where children are no longer allowed to play, stealing girls as prizes for their fighters.

Mouth of the river.

As the Brotherhood builds hospitals, provides food, and educates children, its violent offshoots continue their charge across the Middle East and Africa.

And we leave a void.

There is a truism often heard about old veterans: the most battle hardened are the most likely to wish for peace. Call me a hippie.

Actually, please don't ever call me a hippie, but do understand that my experiences have led to great empathy, not only for those doing what we do, positions no American should have to fill, but for the people in other countries who get caught up in war. I'd be lying if I said the people from the Unit are any less likely to suffer the nightmares, tendency toward drinking, divorce rate, and constant need for an adrenaline kick we've seen in other service members.

If I couldn't remember the number of times I deployed, my wife could—as well as that I missed seven out of ten anniversaries and five out of five Ramadans in the past five years. And that I missed my daughter's first day of school and first birthday.

And birth.

After each deployment, it took me about a month to become normal.

It takes a strong, dedicated spouse to stick with one of us. My wife went through a lot more than I did. I always knew where I was, while she wondered if I was safe.

She kept me alive.

We have seen brothers and sisters from the Unit take their

own lives as they return home. (And, because we don't exist, it's much harder to get Veterans Affairs to approve our claims. Somebody should fix that.)

My time in the military played out in ways I could never have expected—and ways that may seem hard to believe after watching veterans and service members converge on the Capitol on January 6, 2021, in an extreme show of intolerance.

One of my daughters asked me recently why I am so tolerant—why my experiences have not made me suspicious or angry or closed-minded. Many people from the Middle East are pretty conservative, even if they're not extreme in their beliefs.

But being tolerant has, through the years, helped me. I made people feel safe—I made even extremists feel safe, and they talked to me. I was willing to hear them out, to find connections beneath the bullshit, to see if there was a path out of the bullshit. I think because I didn't feel 100 percent accepted by the people I worked with, I feel a sense of compassion to others who may have experienced similar situations. Picture a white guy with a Deep South accent who faces a stereotype that he's slow, rather than that he comes from a culture of storytelling and depth and can build radio equipment out of two shoestrings and a gum wrapper. Picture a guy from Texas who took me home on my first day at my first unit and wanted to know all about the Pyramids. Picture a Jewish guy with a great gift for languages whose religion isn't on his dog tags and who pals around with a short Muslim dude. Picture a well-liked, well-respected, sharp-as-hell woman who never talks about her boyfriend and then finally mentions her girlfriend.

My people.

We were all in it together.

I told my daughter that some of my tolerance comes from luck.

Parents raise their children to be extremists, in all religions—Jewish, Christian, Muslim, Buddhist. People don't necessarily have a choice about their views because either they don't know any other way or they would be ostracized from their communities if they didn't conform.

Those folks might change if they got a chance to see the world from a different optic. But you can't judge a guy who grew up in a cave in Afghanistan.

Thinking about that helped me become more tolerant, more open-minded. I'm sure I have a lot of things wrong with me, but a lot of people still accept me. "Wrong" is probably the, ahem, wrong word—their thoughts just don't match mine. And I've had a lot of aha moments in my life, as well as some beliefs that came about gradually. But it's fair to say my beliefs now are very different from when I first came to this country.

Except that, as a kid, I learned that I was supposed to be kind to my family, to my neighbors, to people who travel through. There are verses from the Quran that teach those lessons. Maybe my experience in the Army and in America just reiterated what I had learned as a child.

Funny story: My mother-in-law visited the United States and saw women who looked like her. They covered their hair. They wore modest skirts. Long sleeves hid their skin. She felt bad she hadn't greeted them.

"They're not Muslim," I said. "They're Jewish."

It would have been difficult to tell the difference between the Orthodox Jews who lived near us in the States and the women I grew up with in Alexandria.

I've also done my part to help people understand my religion. I never proselytized—my mission was always soldiering. But you know how I feel about education.

People have these odd ideas about Islam, but some of it is cultural—not religious. An Indian Muslim has a different day-to-day from an Egyptian Muslim or a Bosnian Muslim or a French Muslim. All of these people have their religion and their culture—just as American Christians, Egyptian Christians, Chinese Christians, and Russian Christians do.

Pakistani Muslims mix their culture and their religion because Islam is a way of life. Is a woman driving a car wrong from a religious standpoint or a cultural standpoint? Are women barred from medical treatment in Afghanistan for religious reasons or cultural reasons? If you grow up in a culture so influenced by religion, you learn that anything that is "wrong" is wrong because your religion bans it—even if that's not the case. Maybe the Prophet Mohammed had a beard because he didn't have a razor, like Jesus and Moses. The Quran doesn't say you can't shave. The Prophet didn't have a car (and probably didn't have a problem with women riding camels) or ride an airplane or wear those supercool white high-top sneakers the Taliban has going on.

There are still ways forward, ways that recognize those cultural differences. Biden could slowly back out of the places we've deconstructed over the past twenty years—but he could then figure out how to fund education for future leaders.

I think of it like a yard full of grass. It looks awful—brown patches and dandelions and spots where the dog kept pissing on it—so you seed up the rough patches. You add some fertilizer. The weeds? They need to be pulled because they're just killing the grass. They're hopeless. But you're thinking long-term, and you're dreaming of that rolling lawn where the kids can play baseball and all of the neighbors can come for beer or mint tea.

Seeds are education. Weeds are extremists.

It will take time to grow the new grass, and the United States won't have the attention span for it. Biden wants to have an impact right away so he can win the next election, and then four years later, he will be out, and then the next person will be in, and they'll want to make an impact so they can win the next election.

In the military, the average command is two years. Commanders aren't going to play out something that goes longer than their tour. They're mostly just making sure they get a good evaluation (or two) so they can tick the boxes to further their career.

The Russians? On some deployments, I've seen Russians who spoke the language of the country. They grew up there—these famous Russian "plants." They live in a place for years. The Russians think long-term. They wait. The United States? Burger King. We want it fast. We send people to language training for a month. A month isn't good enough. To see how a culture, a language, and a religion work in a region, everything needs to be extended, but it takes a long time for the grass to grow, and we're not patient.

There is a quick solution for our military: Bring in the immigrants, the people who came to this country believing they could have a better life. Let them bring their natural cultural training. Let them bring their ability to fit in. Let them bring their ability to educate.

That will take some work. Right now, why would you join the military as an immigrant? Even with promises of citizenship, we saw 250 veterans deported from 2013 to 2018, according to the

Government Accountability Report. They need citizenship, and we need to rebuild that trust.[22]

This won't surprise you: saying no Muslims are allowed into the country doesn't make the Muslims who already live here—and have lived here for years, for generations—feel welcome.

We create a void in the United States, as well, every time we treat an immigrant like an outsider rather than inviting that person in, embracing that person, and helping that person to become a part of the American Dream. Immigrants should be more than a source of low-income labor. Immigrants who believe they are more don't threaten a democracy; they lift it.

I started the final push up Kilimanjaro an hour after everybody else. I knew I would move faster than everybody else. I knew I would rush. I finished in four hours. When I arrived at the top, the wind howled. I felt as if the tip of my nose would break off like an icicle if I touched it. I knew that if I stayed longer than ten to fifteen minutes, my body would run short of oxygen.

I saw shadows sleeping in the snow of the crater. It was beautiful. But it was dark.

Endgame. If I had slowed down a bit, or planned better, or spent more time with the guide, things might have turned out differently.

I caught sunrise on the way back down.

---

22 Karli Goldenberg, "'Fighting on All Fronts': Deported US Veterans Cautiously Optimistic Biden Will Bring Them Home," Medill News Service, Military.com, April 10, 2021, https://www.military.com/daily-news/2021/04/10/fighting-all-fronts-deported-us -veterans-cautiously-optimistic-biden-will-bring-them-home.html.

TWENTY-SEVEN A FOLDED FLAG

MY DAUGHTERS HAVE NO idea what I did in the Army. They also did not know that they were in mind during each deployment. They make me proud every day as I see them growing into strong young Americans, and they are very grateful for the post-9/11 GI Bill, which will cover half of their college education. Because of my wartime deployments, I was able to transfer my GI Bill benefits to them. Thanks to a policy change by President George W. Bush.

One had been a toddler when I was shot and didn't realize it had even happened until two or three years ago.

My wife knows I was in an elite unit, but she didn't know what that elite unit was.

They, and my brother, seemed a bit surprised when four hundred people showed up for my retirement ceremony.

So was I.

I remembered my father, when I left for the United States, telling me I would fail—because that's what his father had told him. I didn't fail.

During the ceremony, my family knew something was up when the top intelligence officer—a three-star general—showed up, as well as another two-star general. My younger daughter mesmerized everyone with her smile while she handled my camera. It was too big for her to carry, but she handled it like a pro.

"I just want you to know there are a lot of things about your dad you don't know," the presiding officer said. "He's a hero." I looked at my wife, and I saw the tears start.

My family was proud, but they didn't quite know why.

I was, and always will be, proud of my family, and they will never quite understand that, either.

My wife supported me in everything I did, and I know it was far more difficult for her than it was for me when I deployed. She managed all our life affairs, as well as raising the two most beautiful daughters. My older daughter was born while I was going through my training. My wife dealt with a newborn baby by herself while I focused on all the special training needed for the Unit. My younger daughter—fireball—was born five years later. She brought a new spark to the family, and that made me dislike leaving my family for deployments even more.

For retirement, I wrote a letter to each of my daughters and then had it engraved and framed with a Bronze Star attached. I also wrote one for my wife, which had my Purple Heart attached. She earned it by keeping up with me during my recovery.

But even as we celebrated, I couldn't take my mind off an analyst I had worked with during my final assignment.

In my last job, the commander and I—I was the sergeant major—worked with about 1,100 soldiers and civilians. One woman, an analyst, requested an overseas assignment. She was French American, born in Sierra Leone. She immigrated to the United States, and then she joined the military and stayed in for eight years. She left the military and worked as a civilian for the Defense Department. She was a white, Christian woman in a white, Christian country.

After her reassignment was approved, she packed her things. She took all of her friends for a goodbye dinner. She cleared her housing. All she had was her backpack. And a gun. She went to her hotel that evening, and she took her own life.

I've never seen a suicide so perfectly executed. She planned it for three years.

As I listened to her eulogy at her service, I thought about how sad it was that she never felt welcomed. Her suicide note said she was tired of not belonging.

If she didn't belong, then how the fuck could I?

Gilmore, in basic training, made sure I knew what a canteen was. Green took me under his wing when I showed up lost at Fort Hood. Pringle recognized my potential and made sure I had good career choices. The guys in the Unit became my best friends—they trusted me with their lives, as I did them with mine.

They gave me the strength to put up with the bullshit but also the motivation to make sure I mentored others.

That's how. That's how I belonged.

But we, as a nation, failed her.

I needed the organization to think about why a white, Christian woman from France felt she did not belong in our military. I wanted them to think about why a guy coming from India—or Afghanistan or Iraq—may not feel as if he belongs. I needed the organization to think, most importantly, about why the military needs them to feel as if they belong.

A lot of people talk about the United States as a melting pot. But I think that takes away the individual flavors—makes everything taste the same. I like to think of us as more of a salad, jumbled together but still bringing individual attributes.

When I left the Unit, I worried not only because I was leaving my guys but because my experience as a Muslim man would come with me. I need two groups to hear my story: Military leadership, so they understand the necessity of diversity. And Muslim Americans—or any immigrant who needs some hope—so they know there's a place that's ready for them and that desperately needs them.

I want to be an inspiration to others. I want people to know the government is not anti-Arab, even if some racism exists within the ranks. I want people to know they can join the FBI and the CIA and the Army. And I want them to know that they can be themselves.

I think of it like being adopted as a young adult. I had my biological country—Egypt—and Egypt did what it could for me with its limited resources. But my adoptive country—America— educated me and gave me dignity and respect and freedom. I will always love Egypt and my culture, but I also love and am loyal to the country that took me in and allowed me to open my mind and be fully myself.

I'm not what you picture when you think about special operations. You're picturing James Bond, or that dude with the facial hair and the Oakleys and the baseball hat with an American flag on it.

I have all that stuff.

But I'm a five-foot-one, 128-pound Muslim guy.

Without my brown skin, without my Muslim upbringing, without my cultural understanding of Africa, I would never have benefited my team—or my country—in the same way.

But my story?

My story is about the American Dream.

ACKNOWLEDGMENTS

I AM IMMENSELY GRATEFUL for the countless individuals who have been instrumental in shaping my journey and helping me reach where I am today. From my teachers who imparted knowledge and wisdom, to my military mentors who instilled discipline and resilience, and to those kind-hearted individuals who offered me a job despite my initial struggles with the English language—each one has played a vital role in my personal and professional growth.

While I deeply appreciate the contributions of all these remarkable people, I must acknowledge and give credit to the *current* and *former* Unit members who have valiantly kept us all out of harm's way. Their unwavering dedication to maintaining the highest level of professionalism while also ensuring the safety and security of our organization is truly commendable.

Protecting the identities of all involved is paramount to the safety and well-being of our organization and its members. Their courage, sacrifices, and commitment to excellence deserve our utmost gratitude and admiration.

In addition, I would like to express my heartfelt gratitude to Kelly, my coauthor; Frank, my agent; and Marc, my publisher and editor. Thank you for believing in me and guiding me through the process. Your support and expertise have been invaluable, and I genuinely appreciate all the help you have provided. I could not have achieved this milestone without each of you by my side.

INDEX

Abdel-Rahman, Omar (Blind
    Sheikh), 23, 24, 53, 54, 55–57
Abu Bakr, 173
Abu Dhabi, UAE, 209–12
Abu Ghraib, 175–77
Afghanistan
    Muslim extremism in, 26
    terrorism in, 4, 172, 192, 194–95
    war in, 22, 25–26
Africa. *See also under* Gamal, Adam,
    in the Unit; *specific countries*
    AG's focus on, 4, 189–90, 192
    extremist ideology in, 192–93, 195
    terrorists trained in, 4, 24, 192,
        194, 195, 201, 207
Ahmadinejad, Mahmoud, 257
Aidid, Mohamed Farrah, 121, 125
airborne school, 117–21

Alexandria, Egypt
    brick walls in, 17, 21
    climate, 47–48
    Jewish population in, 47
    life in, 9, 11–13, 15–16, 25
    Muslim Brotherhood in, 25
Ali, 173
allostatic load, 259
al-Qaeda
    Abu Ghraib and, 176–77
    in East Africa, 213
    formation of, 95, 125
    Muslim Brotherhood and,
        129
    in Pakistan, 207–8
    as recognized threat to US, 125
    scope of network, 164
    in Somalia, 2, 195